W9-AFE-916

INSIGHT GUIDES

NEW ZEALAND
Step by Step

APA PUBLICATIONS
Part of the Langenscheidt Publishing Group

CONTENTS

ABOUT THIS BOOK

This *Step by Step Guide* has been produced by the editors of Insight Guides, whose books have set the standard for visual travel guides since 1970. With top-quality photography and authoritative recommendations, this guidebook brings you the very best of New Zealand in a series of 18 tailor-made tours.

WALKS AND TOURS

The tours in the book provide something to suit all budgets, tastes and trip lengths, so whether you are an architecture buff, a lover of flora and fauna or have kids to entertain, you will find an option to suit. From the subtropical north to the temperate south, all the wonders of the country are presented, with the tours grouped around five geographical hubs: Auckland, Rotorua and Wellington in the North Island and Christchurch and Queenstown in the South Island. There are walking tours of the main city sights as well as day- and multi-day tours of the surrounding areas.

We recommend that you read the whole of a tour before setting out. This should help you to familiarise yourself with the route and enable you to plan where to stop for refreshments – options for this are shown in the 'Food and Drink' boxes, recognisable by the knife and fork sign, on most pages.

For our pick of the walks by theme, consult 'Recommended Tours For…' *(see pp.6–7).*

OVERVIEW

The tours are set in context by this introductory section, which gives an overview of the country to set the scene, plus background information on food and drink and shopping. A succinct history timeline highlights the key events that have shaped New Zealand over the centuries.

DIRECTORY

Also supporting the tours is a Directory chapter, comprising a user-friendly, clearly organised A–Z of practical information, our pick of where to stay while you are in the country, and select restaurant listings; these eateries complement the more low-key cafés and restaurants that feature within the tours themselves and are intended to offer a wider choice for evening dining.

Above: New Zealand highlights.

The Authors

Many of the tours in this guide were originally conceived by **Craig Dowling**, who has lived and worked as a journalist in New Zealand's three largest cities, Auckland, Wellington and Christchurch, gaining a broad insight into the diversity that makes it such an incredible country. The tours have been thoroughly revised and updated for this *Step by Step Guide* by **Donna Blaber**, a travel journalist based in Waipu. Donna has also added a new introductory chapter and new listings for the Directory at the back of the book.

Margin Tips
Shopping tips, historical facts, handy hints and information on activities help visitors to make the most of their time in New Zealand.

Key Facts Box
This box gives details of the distance covered on the tour, plus an estimate of how long it should take. It also states where the route starts and finishes, and gives key travel information, such as which days are best to do the route, or handy transport tips.

Footers
Look here for the tour name, a map reference and the main attraction on the double page.

Food and Drink
Recommendations of where to stop for refreshment are given in these boxes. The numbers prior to each restaurant/café name link to references in the main text. Restaurants in the Food and Drink boxes are plotted on the individual tour maps.

The $ signs at the end of each entry reflect the approximate cost of a two-course meal for one, with one glass of house wine. These should be seen as a guide only. Price ranges, also quoted on the inside back flap for easy reference, are as follows:

$$$$	NZ$80 and above
$$$	NZ$60–80
$$	NZ$40–60
$	NZ$40 and below

Route Map
Detailed cartography shows the tour clearly plotted with numbered dots. For more detailed mapping, see the pull-out map slotted inside the back cover.

ANIMAL LOVERS

Enjoy whale-watching off the coast at Kaikoura (tour 10), visit Akaroa to spot dolphins, fur seals and sea birds (tour 12) and spend a couple of hours at the Kelly Tarlton's aquarium for the low-down on sea life in New Zealand (tour 2).

RECOMMENDED TOURS FOR...

ART LOVERS

The country's main galleries include the Auckland Art Gallery (tour 1) and, in Christchurch (tour 11), the Christchurch Art Gallery and the Centre of Contemporary Art.

CHILDREN

Visit Kelly Tarlton's aquarium (tour 2), watch sheep-shearing at Rainbow Farm in Rotorua (tour 6), look out for seals in the Wairarapa region (tour 9), or make a splash punting in Christchurch (tour 11).

DAREDEVILS

Try rafting waterfalls around Rotorua (tour 5), glacier hiking and ice-climbing on the Franz Josef and Fox glaciers (tour 15) or bungy-jumping where the craze originated, near Queenstown (tours 16 and 17), the self-styled 'Adventure Capital of the World'.

FOOD AND WINE

Enjoy a vineyard tour at Martinborough, the heart of the Marlborough wine industry (tour 9), in the Waipara Valley wine region (tour 13) or at Gibbston Valley Wines (tour 17), near Arrowtown.

GEOTHERMAL ACTIVITY

For spouting geysers, bubbling mud pools and natural hot springs, visit Rotorua (tour 6) or Taupo (tour 7).

HISTORY HUNTERS

Retrace the past at Auckland's War Memorial Museum (tour 1), in Northland, the birthplace of the nation and home to the country's founding document, the Treaty of Waitangi (tour 3) and at the Museum of New Zealand in Wellington (tour 8).

PAMPERING

Take time out in your own freshly dug warm pool on Hot Water Beach (tour 4), at Rotorua's Polynesian Spa (tour 6), in a hot salt-water pool near Mount Maunganui (tour 5) and at Hanmer Springs Thermal Resort and Spa (tour 13).

SPORTY TYPES

Try your hand at yachting or watch the All Blacks in Auckland (tour 1), partake in the 'Round the Bays' run in the Bay of Islands (tour 2) or surf near Whangamata (tour 4).

UNBEATABLE VIEWS

There are so many unbeatable views in New Zealand that it's hard to summarise, but highlights include the views around Aoraki/Mount Cook, the country's highest mountain (tour 14), the scenery around the Franz Josef and Fox glaciers (tour 15) and around Milford Sound (tour 18).

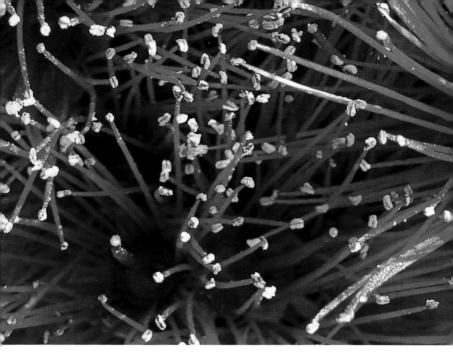

• WAIRARAPA EEL
• KAPITI CHEESE
• COROMANDEL SMOKED
  SEAFOOD
• BLACK
  PUDDING

OVERVIEW

An overview of New Zealand's geography, customs and culture, plus illuminating background information on food and drink, shopping and history.

COUNTRY OVERVIEW

New Zealand's archipelago of around 700 islands offers a wealth of dramatic scenery, from the exquisite beauty of Milford Sound to the bush-wrapped solitude of Lake Waikaremoana and the boiling surprises of the thermal regions.

Local Birdlife
New Zealand's unique birds include the flightless kiwi *(above, top)*, the unofficial national symbol, from which its inhabitants take their nickname. It has hair-like feathers and a long, slender bill. Kiwi birds are only active at night in wilderness areas. The country's cheekiest feathered friend is the kea *(above, bottom)*, an alpine parrot, renowned for its fearlessness of humans. Other flightless birds include the weka and the endangered kakapo, the world's largest parrot.

New Zealand is situated in the South Pacific between latitudes 34° and 37° South. It is a long, narrow country, lying roughly north–south and comprising two main islands – the North and the South – separated by the Cook Strait. It is surrounded by the Pacific Ocean on its east coast and the Tasman Sea on its west coast. At 269,057 sq km (103,883 sq miles), it is slightly larger than the British Isles. Two-thirds of the country is mountainous and dissected by swift-flowing rivers, deep alpine lakes and subtropical forest. Its highest mountain is Aoraki/Mount Cook, located in the Southern Alps.

Meteoric Rise to Fame

New Zealand's remoteness from the rest of the world has served both to limit the number of visitors and to preserve the land from over-exploitation. Those who did come were delighted by what they found packed into a comparatively small country. But what was known to only a number of enthusiasts became known to millions in 2001, with the release of the movie *The Lord of the Rings: The Fellowship of the Ring*, directed by native son Peter Jackson. Cast in the role of Middle Earth, New Zealand's spectacular landscapes became travel's worst-kept secret.

GETTING AROUND

For the independent traveller, New Zealand's geography, while providing scenes of unsurpassed beauty, poses some difficulties in terms of time. The country's length and rough-hewn nature, plus the division into two main islands, makes travelling time often longer than you expect. The bottom-line is that when your vacation time is limited, it is impossible to see everything the country has to offer.

Most of the tours in this book focus on five main hubs – Auckland, Rotorua, Wellington, Christchurch and Queenstown – with a number of additional tours guiding you around the attractions in the rest of the country (the historic Bay of Islands; the beautiful beaches of Coromandel Peninsula; the adventure activities of Lake Taupo; the wineries of Wairarapa; the stunning glaciers of the South Island's West Coast; and the majesty of Milford Sound). If time allows, the tours can be linked together for an extensive north–south, or south–north, exploration of the whole country.

Travel Tips

If time is at a premium, it may help to use domestic flights to travel between

the main city hubs, then hire a car to access regional attractions. With its quiet, well-maintained roads, New Zealand is the perfect destination to tour by car. New Zealanders take seriously their commitment to protecting, as well as making accessible, the beauty of their natural environment.

NORTH ISLAND

Auckland and Northland

In subtropical Northland, proud forests of majestic kauri trees, some thousands of years old, share space with its gumdigging past. Gnarled red-blossoming pohutukawa trees (known as New Zealand Christmas trees) cling to windswept cliffs over golden beaches, and green rolling hills of farmland span from coast to coast. Thermal activity abounds: there's Auckland, built on extinct volcanos; Rotorua, famous for its intense thermal activity in the form of geysers, hot springs and pools of boiling mud; and one of New Zealand's most special experiences: digging your own warm spa in the sand at the Coromandel's Hot Water Beach *(see p.45)*.

Lake Taupo and Wellington

At the heart of the North Island lies Lake Taupo *(see p.57)*, New Zealand's largest lake: a huge volcanic crater fed by the mountains of the Central Plateau. Hidden beneath hills beside a crater-formed harbour, the capital city of Wellington is the departure point to the magnificent South Island, home to only one quarter of the country's population.

SOUTH ISLAND

The South Island provides travellers with an awe-inspiring panorama of majestic snowy mountains, dripping rainforest, silent fiords and sounds, ancient glaciers, wide open plains and sparkling blue lakes and rivers. This is a place of grandeur and solitude, where visitors really can become at one with nature, in the shadow of the Southern Alps. These mountains, a spine of jagged peaks running the length of the South Island, were formed by a collision of tectonic plates, which, in a bid to outdo each other, force the mountains upwards by some 10mm ($\frac{1}{5}$in) per year.

As it is, the Southern Alps rise to heights of over 3,000m (9,843ft) in places, with Aoraki/Mount Cook, New Zealand's highest mountain, dominating the range at 3,750m (12,303ft).

Above from far left: Pohutukawa tree; Rere Falls, near Gisborne, in the East Cape (North Island); extreme mountain biking in the Southern Alps (South Island); wine country in the Canterbury region of the South Island.

Green Philosophy
The Maori story of creation explains that land and human beings are all one – flesh and clay from the same source material. The indigenous Maori emotional attachment to place is profound and has influenced *Pakeha* (European) culture, contributing to the national belief that 'clean and green' is a philosophy, not just a tourism marketing tool.

Left: footprints on the beach.

Above: bungy-
jumpers at The
Swoop in Rotorua;
cute New Zealand
lambs; Lake Wanaka
on the South Island.

Poisonous Critters
New Zealand has no
snakes or dangerous
wild animals, making
it safe, in that respect,
for visitors to enjoy
outdoor activities.

The West Coast

The West Coast offers a wealth of contrasting scenery, from dense forests of beech, to deep fiords and the icy tongues of Franz Josef and Fox glaciers *(see p.90–1)*, while the picturesque lakeside townships of Wanaka, Queenstown and Te Anau provide a base for adventure in the great outdoors.

To the east, the genteel city of Christchurch *(see p.71)* is attractively set amid patchwork plains and beautiful gardens beside the clear waters of the Avon River.

CLIMATE AND SEASONS

New Zealand's climate ranges from subtropical in the Northland to temperate/cool in the deep south. Places such as Invercargill on the southern coast of the South Island can be bitterly cold in winter, when southerly winds blow up from Antarctica. In terms of seasons, summer runs from December to February, autumn from March to May, winter from June to August, and spring from September to November.

Clothing

Whatever the season, it's essential to bring umbrellas and waterproofs, as a typical day in Auckland alternates between showers and sun. In the South Island, Fiordland and the West Coast have very high rainfall – Milford Sound gets over 6m (20ft) of rain a year.

Alpine weather is notoriously changeable, so those planning on visiting mountainous regions should bring plenty of warm clothing, even in summer. Take broken-in walking boots if you're planning on doing any hiking.

Dress is generally casual, although some pubs and hotel bars frown on jeans, jandals (flip-flops) or sandals, and bare feet, and some request that men wear ties.

ACTIVITIES

Given New Zealand's diverse, remarkable terrain, it's not surprising that outdoor activities are huge business here. The following is a brief description of the main ones; for more information, visit the Tourism New Zealand website: www.newzealand.com.

Bungy-Jumping and Skydiving

New Zealand is where the craze for bungy-jumping began, and you can still throw yourself off a ledge with a rubber band attached to your ankles at many (often spectacular) places across the country. If jumping from a ledge with a rubber band tied to your leg is too passé for you, how about a tandem skydive? The bonus with this thrill is the stunning view offered by the plane ride as you circle up above the drop zone.

Fishing, Dolphins and Whales

New Zealand's waters are a breeding ground for a variety of native and introduced fish species, notably trout and salmon, as well as big game, and the country is well regarded for the angling opportunities it presents. Whether you hire a guide or head out on your own, you're assured of a good catch.

Get up close and personal with dol-

phins at several locations around the country, by hopping aboard a boat tour. Whales-watching tours are available in Kaikoura *(see p. 70)*.

Jet-Boating and Rafting

Swift-flowing and broad, shallow rivers meant that traditional boats were next to useless in many of New Zealand's waterways. A new type of vessel – the jet-boat – was consequently developed here. Visitors can hop aboard for thrilling high-speed rides at several locations nationwide.

Another great way to experience New Zealand's fast-flowing rivers is in a raft. Rivers range from grade 1 (easy) to grade 5 (extreme), and trips vary from a few hours to a few days.

Snowsports

The rugged terrain offers a wide range of skiing in winter, typically at much lower prices than in Europe or the US. North Island commercial ski fields include Whakapapa and Turoa, both on the slopes of Mount Ruapehu, while in the South Island Queenstown offers a range of fields within easy reach, as does the city of Christchurch.

LANGUAGE

New Zealand has two official languages, English and Maori. Nearly everyone speaks English (with a distinctive, often nasal accent). New Zealand has adopted standard English grammar and spelling, but has also added some 'Kiwi-isms' to the vocabulary. You may hear, for instance, the

word 'grotty', meaning dirty; or 'chilly bin', a portable cooler used for picnics; or 'grog', for alcohol.

Maori

Maori is a language undergoing a renaissance. It is taught in schools and is commonly spoken as a first language in some parts of the North Island. Maori influence is strong throughout the country in place names, and many words have entered common usage, for example: *Pakeha*, meaning a person of European descent; *kia ora*, for hello; *kai*, for food; *koha*, if a donation is required; and *hangi*, a style of Maori cooking.

Pronunciation is not difficult, once you master the vowels, which often occur alongside each other but are pronounced separately: a as in car; o like 'aw' in 'paw'; i like 'ea' in 'bean'; e as in 'men'; u like oo in 'moon'. The only complex sounds are wh, pronounced more or less like 'f', and ng, pronounced like the 'ing' in 'singing'. Syllables are given equal stress. Maori words do not take an 's' to form the plural.

The Ultimate Linguistic Test

If you feel that you've gained a certain proficiency in the Maori language, try one of the longest place names in the world, attached to a hill in the Hawke's Bay area. In its shortened version it's called Taumatawhakatangihangako-auauotamateapokaiwhenuakitanatahu. It means, 'Where Tamatea of the big knees, the man who slid down, climbed and consumed mountains and is known as the land-eater, played the flute to his beloved'.

Geology

New Zealand's separation from other land masses about 100 million years ago allowed many ancient plants and animals to survive and evolve in isolation. For this reason its landscape features an unrivalled variety of landforms, as well as unique flora and fauna.
In a couple of days' driving it is possible to see everything from mountain ranges and sandy beaches to lush rainforests, active volcanoes, glaciers, sounds and fiords.

Government

New Zealand is a sovereign, independent democratic state and a member of both the United Nations and the Commonwealth. The government is elected every three years under the proportional representation system called MMP. The Government's leader is the Prime Minister, while the Head of State is the Queen of England, who is represented here by a resident Governor-General.

FOOD AND DRINK

Kiwi cooking is distinguished by ingredients that are fresh and flavourful, and a style that fuses a medley of influences, reflecting the country's cultural diversity. A latecomer to the world of winemaking, it now also produces outstanding vintages that are sold and acclaimed worldwide.

Above: kiwifruit; crayfish is a delicacy.

Fresh and vibrant, New Zealand's cuisine is often described as Pacific Rim, as it draws much of its inspiration from Europe, Asia and Polynesia. This blend of influences has created a mouth-watering range of flavours and food that can be sampled in cafés, restaurants and lodges nationwide. Innovative chefs make clever use of tasty ingredients freshly harvested from the garden, land and sea – which, in the company of award-winning local wines, make the New Zealand gastronomic experience among the best in the world.

While food and beverage production has long been the linchpin of New Zealand's prosperity and a leading export earner, it's the fusion of unique, quality produce and ethnic influences that has allowed a national food identity to evolve. Nowadays New Zealand's worldwide reputation for award-winning produce draws visitors from afar to the source, and food tourism is developing at a rapid rate.

TRADITIONAL DINING

The country's cuisine culture is also distinctive in the way that New Zealanders prefer to eat; an environment that is as relaxed and unaffected as possible, in tune with the laidback Kiwi psyche.

Cooking Class
If tasting the delights of New Zealand cuisine isn't enough, you can also learn to cook the Kiwi way. Cooking classes are becoming popular, and courses include Catherine Bell's Epicurean Workshop in Auckland and Ruth Pretty's Wellington countryside school, both of which attract foodies from far and wide.

Summer usually means endless barbecues and alfresco dining, with the emphasis on fresh, simple fare. Barbecues have long been a big part of the Kiwi culture, and Pacific influences, organics or home-grown produce, and indigenous foods make it unique. Fare such as lamb, venison, fresh fish including crayfish (lobster) and other shellfish such as pipi, tuatua and scallops, are fresh-harvested and plentiful.

The Hangi

For an authentic New Zealand eating experience, try a traditional Maori *hangi* (pronounced 'hung-ee'), cooked underground. A deep hole is dug, then lined with red-hot stones and covered with vegetation. The food (chicken, pork, lamb, potatoes, kumara – sweet potato – and other vegetables) is placed on top, then the whole 'oven' is sprinkled with water and sealed, and left to steam for several hours, giving a smoky taste.

Traditionally, all members of a *whanau* (family) come for the feast, with stereotypical gender roles the norm: the men digging and working on the hole, and the women preparing the food to go in it. Several tourist locations, including Rotorua in the North Island, invite visitors to join in and experience *hangi* culture (see p.53).

SEAFOOD

Fish is abundant and of very good quality in New Zealand, with varieties including freshwater salmon, sole and flounder. If you want to eat trout, however, note that you will have to catch your own, as it is illegal to sell it *(see p.57)*. Whitebait, a tiny minnow-like fish, is a seasonal delicacy, and can be enjoyed nationwide, although it has become synonymous with the South Island's West Coast.

On your travels, look out for roadside stalls selling succulent crayfish and/or freshly smoked mussels or fish. The sublime flavour of crayfish can also be enjoyed at any good seafood restaurant; try White Morph (Kaikoura, South Island) or Hammerheads (Tamaki Drive, Auckland).

In the summer, shellfish such as mussels, pipi and tuatua are often gathered from the beach. Green-lipped mussels, paua (abalone) and oysters – the Pacific oyster, the rock oyster and the famed Bluff oyster – can also be found on menus nationwide.

British visitors may be pleased to learn that fish and chips are a popular takeaway meal in New Zealand, served in the traditional way: piping hot and wrapped in paper.

NATIONAL SPECIALITIES

Your New Zealand culinary experience is incomplete until you savour the sweet, creamy stickiness of pavlova, the national dessert. In addition, it's worth looking out for some food products that offer an entirely new taste sensation. These include hokey pokey ice cream (vanilla ice cream with toffee bits in it),

Above from far left:
New Zealand lamb; mussels; specials board; fresh salmon.

Markets
Many New Zealanders do part of their main weekly shop at their local farmers' market, making the most of reasonably priced seasonal produce and home-made preserves. Hand-made cheeses, artisan breads, natural ice cream, hand-crafted chocolates, gourmet meats and organic coffee are also often up for grabs.

Below: market-fresh organic produce.

Above: Hokitika is known for its annual Wild Foods Festival, although it's not for the faint-hearted.

L&P soft drink (short for 'Lemon and Paeroa', a lemon-flavoured sparkling drink), jaffas (orange-flavoured sweets), pineapple lumps (candy), tamarillos (tree tomatoes) and feigoas (fruit) and chocolate 'fish'.

Indigenous treats include kumara, a type of sweet potato commonly eaten throughout New Zealand and an essential part of any Sunday roast, and Huhu grubs, found in backyards nationwide, but usually only served at local wild foods festivals.

FOOD FESTIVALS

Food festivals are regularly held throughout the nation, but when it comes to wild cuisine, there's no better place to start than Hokitika. This West Coast town leads the way in untamed gastronomic creativity, with all manner of culinary delights up for grabs during the annual Wild Foods Festival, held to celebrate the harvest.

Stallholders provide crowds with a variety of bizarre tucker, from crickets and huhu grubs to bull's penis and pig's ears and even worm sushi. The less adventurous are not forgotten, however, with gourmet treats such as rabbit pâté, pickled seaweed, ostrich pie, crayfish, whitebait and home-made ice cream also available.

Wine and food festivals are held annually in Auckland, Hawke's Bay, Martinborough, Blenheim, Canterbury and Queenstown, and these national and regional events highlight the production of a wide-ranging supply of gourmet foods and boutique wines.

WINE

Needless to say, New Zealand wines are the only complement to the local cuisine that visitors should consider during their stay. It all began at the top of the country in the Bay of Islands, with James Busby, official British Resident, horticulturist extraordinaire, pioneer viticulturist (he also founded the wine industry in New South Wales, Australia) and author of the Treaty of Waitangi. He planted the first vineyard on his property at Waitangi in the Bay of Islands in 1834, and a couple of years later the very first New Zealand wine was produced. It was sampled by French admiral Dumont d'Urville, who pronounced it to be light, sparkling and delicious.

Matakana, just north of Auckland, and associated vineyards in the Kaipara region were the first to attempt serious commercial wine-making – in the last quarter of the 18th century – but suffered from the scourge of prohibition politics that effectively destroyed the wine industry between 1900 and 1920. Now enjoying an optimistic revival, this pretty rural area produces some of New Zealand's classiest wines and most visitor-friendly wineries, notably Heron's Flight (www.heronsflight.co.nz), with its garden dining and delightfully casual attitude.

International Standing

If New Zealand has a signature wine, it is sauvignon blanc. Saint Clair Estate Wines (www.saintclair.co.nz) in

Marlborough was named the maker of the best sauvignon blanc in the world at the 2006 San Francisco International Wine Competition, America's largest and most prestigious competition. The award-winning wine was its Vicar's Choice Sauvignon Blanc 2006.

Also in the running as the country's signature wine is pinot noir. The Black Poplar Block Pinot Noir 2003 from Central Otago's Pisa Range Estate (www.pisarangeestate.co.nz) won a gold medal (best in class) in the 37th International Wine and Spirit Competition in London. Even more noteworthy is that the label was only launched in 2002. One expert has also predicted a syrah (known in Australia and New Zealand as shiraz) revolution.

PLACES TO EAT

Most major towns and cities have a range of eateries, from food courts to cafés, casual restaurants and brasseries, through to high-class establishments. Like everything, you will get what you pay for, but it is fair to say that there is a trend towards a lighter and healthier style of cooking, with a focus on fresh New Zealand produce. Likewise, cafés are increasingly replacing the tearooms of old. Most restaurants/cafés offer at least one or two vegetarian and/or gluten-free dishes on their menu.

Cafés open as early as 7am, while most restaurants tend to commence service around 6pm, with last orders taken around 10pm. Note that in smaller towns it's best to book, as restaurants will close early – or not open at all – if they think they have no patrons.

Many restaurants are licensed, and BYO (Bring Your Own) places – licensed for the consumption and not the sale of alcohol – are also popular. Feel free to take along bottles of wine, but note that bringing your own beer is frowned upon.

Above from far left: fresh, light food is fashionable; on the Hawke's Bay wine trail; dining alfresco at Huka Lodge *(see p.114).*

Below: New Zealand is famous for its sauvignon blanc.

SHOPPING

Trade in your New Zealand dollars for, among other things, hand-crafted Maori carvings, pretty jade and iridescent paua-shell jewellery, hand-made pottery and, of course, woolly jumpers and sheepskin goods.

Above: pretty *paua* shell; pottery shoes.

Walk of Fame

At Victoria Park Market look out for the Celebrity Walk of Fame, located on the old horse ramp that leads between the stable buildings and the courtyard. Here, the hand- or footprints of New Zealand's most outstanding modern-day achievers including Sir Edmund Hillary, Dame Kiri Te Kanawa and comedian Billy T. James are immortalised in cement.

New Zealand offers a huge variety of shopping from arts and craft markets, gallery and museum shops to exclusive designer stores. For traditional New Zealand souvenirs look for hand-crafted Maori carvings in wood, bone and *pounamu* (greenstone or jade). You can also find jewellery and ornaments made from the iridescent *paua* shell (abalone), treasured by Maori for centuries.

New Zealand potters are among the world's finest, and today many fine artisans are also working in stone, wood, glass and metals. With over 40 million sheep, it is no surprise that the country's wool industry is going strong; wonderful hand-knitted wool sweaters, beautiful wall hangings, homespun yarns and top-quality sheepskins are plentiful. New Zealand also has 70 million possums (culled as this introduced species are damaging to the environment), so expect to see possum-skin goods, too.

Alongside top international fashion in the main city areas, you will also find New Zealand's own fashion labels, including Zambesi, NomD, Karen Walker and World.

WHERE TO BUY

Auckland
New Zealand's largest city offers some of the country's most varied retail therapy. Queen Street is the hub for souvenir shopping, with 'downtown' Queen Street hosting the major duty-free stores. For a full range of items, try the DFS Galleria on the corner of Customs Street and Albert Street. Vulcan Lane, off Queen Street, leads to High Street and the Chancery District, where Auckland's major designer fashion boutiques are clustered.

For a completely different shopping experience, go to Victoria Park Market (daily 9am–6pm), recognisable by its large red-brick chimney, on Victoria Street West, where a huge variety of goods from leatherware through to pottery are on offer; there are cafés in the complex, too.

Rotorua
The main shopping street in Rotorua is Tutanekai Street, although several souvenir shops are on Fenton Street, close to the Visitor Centre. Maori arts and craft abound in here, as do leather and sheepskin products. The Best of Maori Tourism (corner of Fenton and Haupapa streets) offers original Maori-designed clothing and carvings in bone and wood. Craftspeople can be watched while they work at The Jade Factory (1288 Fenton Street), and at the New Zealand Maori Arts and Crafts Institute at Whakarewarewa.

Wellington

Shopping in the capital city centres around Lambton Quay and ranges from high-street chains such as Farmers, through to clothing chain stores including Country Road and Max. Bookstores including Whitcoulls and Dymocks are good places to pick up holiday reading.

For crafts and antiques, spend an hour or two browsing the converted villas of Tinakori Road. If you prefer less mainstream fashions, the small designer clothing stores that compete for space with second-hand bookshops along Cuba Street are recommended. Also worth a visit is Wellington institution Kirkaldie and Staines; located at 165–77 Lambton Quay, this department store is renowned for its quality products and good old-fashioned service.

Christchurch

For inner-city shopping Christchurch's best bet is the pedestrian-only Cashel Mall, where home-grown boutique fashion stores such as Flame, Workshop and Plume compete with international brands such as Esprit.

Christchurch's best-known department store, Ballantynes, is located on the corner of Cashel Mall and Colombo Street, and the city has several duty-free outlets located on the north side of Cathedral Square. DFS and Regency Duty-Free both have outlets at the airport, where a range of clothing boutiques, gift stores and bookshops cater to last-minute shoppers.

To find something a little bit different, head to the Arts Centre on Worcester Boulevard. Here you will find a variety of handcrafted gift ideas, plus an ever-changing range of antiques and prints.

Queenstown

Queenstown aims to please its visitors in every way possible – including shopping – with many stores open for extended hours on a daily basis, so you can buy just about anything, at any time. Jewellery, duty-free and artisan stores line The Mall, while O'Connells Shopping Centre, at the corner of Camp Street and Beach Street hosts around 25 stores under one roof including New Zealand's largest Canterbury of New Zealand store. It sells a wide range of All Blacks and rugby-inspired clothing.

Queenstown's focus on outdoors pursuits is strongly reflected in its wealth of high-quality sportswear apparel shops and sports equipment shops which can be found all over town *(see margin tip, right)*.

PRACTICALITIES

The majority of shops and businesses open 9am to 5pm, Monday to Friday, but many stores also open on Saturday and Sunday, especially in the large cities. In resort areas, too, you will find shops open in the evenings, until around 9pm. It's worth noting that in some places you may experience problems if your credit card uses 'Smart Card' technology; contact your card provider for further information prior to travelling to New Zealand.

Above from far left: traditional Maori textile; detail of a sheepskin rug; carved jade pendant with woven bag.

Book Stores
Book worms will be right at home in New Zealand; the nation has more bookshops per head of population than any other country in the world – one for every 7,500 people.

Outdoor Gear
New Zealanders love the great outdoors, so it should come as little surprise that they have developed a wide range of hard-wearing clothing and equipment to match tough environmental demands. Warm and rugged farm-wear such as Swanndri bush shirts and jackets are popular purchases, while mountaineering equipment, camping gear and backpacks set world standards. Some items have even become fashion success stories, such as the Canterbury range of rugby and yachting jerseys.

HISTORY: KEY DATES

From early days as a Polynesian settlement and the arrival of the Maori to European rule and, finally, independence. The list below covers important social and political events in the history of New Zealand.

Woodcarving
The New Zealand forests contained larger trees than Polynesians would previously have seen. This enabled them to build bigger-than-ever dugout canoes and resulted in a fine tradition of woodcarving.

Early Tourism
The North Island's spas and hot pools earned an early reputation for their curative powers. As early as 1901, the government hired an official balneologist and formed a tourist department, the first government-sponsored tourism promotion organisation in the world.

DISCOVERY

1000	First Polynesian settlers.
1642	Discovery by Abel Tasman.
1769	Captain James Cook's first exploration of New Zealand.

19TH CENTURY

1814	Reverend Samuel Marsden establishes an Anglican mission station.
1826	Attempt at European settlement under Captain Herd.
1840	Arrival of New Zealand Company's settlers. New Zealand annexed by New South Wales. Treaty of Waitangi is signed.
1841	New Zealand proclaimed independent of New South Wales.
1845	'Northern War' between Maori and *Pakeha* (Europeans).
1852	Constitution Act passed. New Zealand divided into six provinces.
1854	First session of the General Assembly in Auckland.
1860	'Taranaki War' between *Pakeha* and Maori.
1861	Gold discovery in Otago. First electric telegraph line opens.
1863	First steam railway opens.
1865	Seat of government transferred to Wellington.
1870	New Zealand's first rugby match. Last battles of 'New Zealand Wars'.
1876	Provincial governments abolished.
1882	First shipment of frozen meat from New Zealand.
1886	Mount Tarawera erupts.
1893	Universal female suffrage is introduced.

20TH CENTURY

1907	The country is granted Dominion status.
1908	North Island main trunk railway opens. Ernest Rutherford awarded Nobel Prize for Chemistry.
1914–18	World War I. Gallipoli campaign by ANZAC troops.
1918	Influenza epidemic.
1931	Hawkes Bay earthquake.

1935	First New Government elected.
1939–45	World War II. New Zealand Division serves in Italy.
1947	Statute of Westminster adopted by Parliament.
1949	National Government elected.
1951	Prolonged waterfront industrial dispute. New Zealand signs ANZUS Treaty alliance with US and Australia.
1953	The Auckland-born mountaineer and explorer Sir Edmund Hillary successfully climbs Mount Everest.
1965	Troops sent to Vietnam.
1967	Decimal system introduced.
1972	Labour Government elected.
1974	Christchurch hosts the Commonwealth Games.
1975	Waitangi Tribunal established to hear Maori land-rights issues. National Government elected.
1981	Tour of New Zealand by South African rugby team leads to riots.
1983	Closer Economic Relations (CER) agreement with Australia.
1984	Labour Government elected. New Zealand becomes nuclear-free.
1985	Greenpeace protest vessel *Rainbow Warrior* bombed by French agents in New Zealand.
1986	Goods and Services Tax (GST) is introduced.
1990	Auckland hosts the Commonwealth Games. National Party wins general election.
1993	Electoral system changed to a proportional system called MMP.
1994	New Zealand wins America's Cup yachting regatta in San Diego.
1995	Waikato's Tainui tribe settles a longstanding grievance claim.
1996	First MMP election. National Party forms coalition government with a minor party, New Zealand First.
1999	New Zealand hosts APEC summit and America's Cup yachting regatta. Labour Party coalition wins elections. Helen Clark becomes Prime Minister (PM).

21ST CENTURY

2002	Labour Party's Helen Clark is returned for a second term as PM.
2003	Team New Zealand loses the America's Cup in Auckland. New Zealand population reaches 4 million. The final instalment of Peter Jackson's *The Lord of the Rings* world premières in Wellington.
2004	The film *The Lord of the Rings: The Return of the King* wins all 11 Academy Awards for which it was nominated.
2007	Sir Edmund Hillary passes away. The nation goes into mourning.
2008	Election year.

Above from far left: signing the Treaty of Waitangi; driving sheep in the 1920s.

Women's Rights
New Zealand has always taken pride in the fact that in 1893 it became the first country in the world to give women the vote, and at the start of the 21st century the prominence of women in public life suggested a developed degree of equality. Arguably the three top positions in the country – Prime Minister, Governor-General and Chief Justice – have been held by women; the second-, third- and fifth-biggest cities have had women mayors; and the chief executive officers of the two major telecommunications companies and biggest bank were women. However, statistics indicate that the median wage for women remains less than that enjoyed by men.

WALKS AND TOURS

AUCKLAND

The country's largest city sits between the harbours of Waitemata and Manukau on an isthmus dotted with extinct volcanoes. This walking tour takes in its key sights, including Auckland Domain, Parnell and the Sky Tower.

Harbour Bridge
The Auckland Harbour Bridge opened on 30 May 1959. The construction took 200 workers, around four years, 6,500 tonnes of concrete and nearly 6,000 tonnes of steel. A few years later 'clippons' (made in Japan) were added to cope with the increasing volume of traffic; they were attached with huge steel pins and rods. To explore the length and breadth of the bridge, take a Bridgeclimb (Westhaven Reserve; tel: 09 361 2000; www. aucklandbridgeclimb. co.nz; daily; charge), which offers an optional bungy jump on the way down.

DISTANCE 7km (4½ miles)
TIME A full day
START Viaduct Harbour
END Sky Tower
POINTS TO NOTE
There is much ground to cover on this route, and you can take bus or taxi rides between key points of interest to spare your feet and save some time along the way, if you want. Another option is to board the Auckland Explorer Bus (tel: 09 571 3119; www.explorerbus.co.nz; charge), a hop-on/hop-off tour featuring many of the sights on this and the next tour; the bus departs from the Ferry Building on Quay Street and runs hourly from 9am throughout the day.

Sandwiched between twin harbours and built on 48 extinct volcanoes, Auckland has long been New Zealand's prime gateway and largest city. Its population topped 1 million a few years ago, and growth is proceeding at a pace that indicates one in three New Zealanders will live there within 10 years. Auckland has the largest Polynesian population of any city in the world; it also has a growing Asian presence. Scenic areas such as the Waitakere

Ranges to the west, the Hunua Ranges to the south, and Waiwera, Okura and Puhoi to the north will be maintained as green belts and hence protected from development.

City of Sails

To the west of Auckland are the shallow waters of the Manukau Harbour, navigable only to small ships. The Waitemata Harbour to the east is a 'Sea of Sparkling Water', indented with bays and scattered with islands' one of them, Rangitoto, an active volcano until just 200 years ago, stands guard at the harbour entrance (for more on Rangitoto, *see tour 2, p.33*).

To the Maori people, the area was *Tamaki-makau-rau*, 'the place of a hundred lovers'. British administrators renamed it, rather less poetically, after an English admiral. Auckland has long since dropped its colonial sobriquet of 'Queen City' and now prefers 'City of Sails'. It is said to possess the world's highest number of boats per head of population, and it certainly looks that way each January, during the Anniversary Day yachting regatta, the world's largest one-day event. The race celebrates the foundation of the city in 1840 as capital of the country – a title it lost 25 years later to Wellington.

VIADUCT HARBOUR

This tour of the city begins downtown at the **Viaduct Harbour ❶**, where **Mecca**, see ⑪①, is a good place for breakfast. After strolling along the waterfront, exit the harbour at the Quay Street archway, where a large suspended yacht, a legacy of New Zealand's endeavours in the America's Cup regatta, is on display. For a taste of America's Cup action, pop into Sail NZ (Viaduct Harbour; www. sailing nz.co.nz), which organises thrilling trips aboard *NZL40* and *NZL41*. Take

Above from far left: the city by night; racing yachts at full speed near Auckland.

Food and Drink 🍴

① **MECCA**
85–7 Customs Street West, Viaduct Harbour; tel: 09 358 1093; $$
Café classics, tasty breakfasts and excellent coffee. Indoor and outdoor seating and harbour views. Breakfast and lunch only.

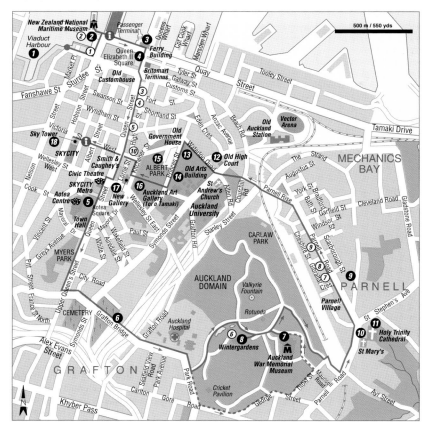

the helm, give it a blast on the grinders or just sit back and enjoy the sights.

Maritime Museum

For an insight into New Zealand's maritime history, check out the nearby **New Zealand National Maritime Museum** ❷ (Princes Wharf; tel: 09 373 0800; www.nzmaritime.org; daily, summer 9am–6pm, winter 9am–5pm; charge), just by the waterfront. The museum showcases boats of all types and is home to the **Waterfront Café**, see ⑪②. At

weekends (11am–3pm), you can take a 20-minute trip around the harbour on the historic steamboat SS *Pike*.

Visitor Information Centre and Ferry Building

From the museum, take a stroll along the waterfront, passing the **Visitor Information Centre** (137 Quay Street, Princes Wharf; tel: 0800 282 552; Mon–Fri 8.30am–6pm, Sat–Sun 8.30am–5pm) en route to the historic **Ferry Building** ❸ at 99 Quay Street. Erected in 1912 to house the offices of harbour officials, this red-brick edifice is now the focal point for commuter ferries that link Auckland with the North Shore and the islands of the Waitemata Harbour and Hauraki Gulf. (Board from the back of the building.)

QUEEN STREET

Cross Quay Street to the fully paved **Queen Elizabeth II Square** ❹, the home of the Britomart Train Terminus, one of the city's key public transport interchanges and the base of Queen Street, the city's main shopping area. Stroll along Queen Street, exploring side streets (home to pitstops including **Revive**, see ⑪③, and the **Vulcan Café**, see ⑪④) and eventually leading to the High Street, with boutique and designer stores and the fashionable **Foodoo**, see ⑪⑤.

Further up on the right at 253–61 Queen Street, you will pass the department store **Smith & Caughey's** (tel: 09 377 4770; www.smithandcaughey.co.nz) and the historic **Civic Theatre**

(corner of Queen Street and Wellesley Street; www. civictheatre.co.nz), which hosts many of Auckland's premier events. Just beyond is the SKYCITY entertainment complex *(see p.32)*, where you can view the latest blockbusters or browse the books at Borders bookstore in the same building.

AOTEA SQUARE

The adjacent **Aotea Square** ❺ has several points of interest. The first is the elaborately carved Maori **Waharoa** (gateway); a symbolic entrance to the square, it stands in stark contrast to the surrounding mirrored-glass buildings. Across Aotea Square is Auckland's main cultural venue, **Aotea Centre** (tel: 09 309 2677; www.the-edge.co.nz). In the foyer you can find out about current and upcoming events, and purchase tickets. On Fridays and Saturdays between 10am and 6pm, the **Aotea Square Market** (tel: 09 307 5377) comes alive with stalls selling funky streetwear, jewellery, food and assorted bric-a-brac.

Bordering the square are City Council buildings, including the renovated **Town Hall** (tel: 09 309 2677; recognisable by its angular form and the clock tower on the eastern fringe.

AUCKLAND DOMAIN

From here, the next destination is Auckland Domain, New Zealand's oldest park. To get there, you can walk, catch a bus (the Link bus from Queen Street) or hail a taxi. This journey of about 1km (½ mile) will take you over

Grafton Bridge ❻ and past Auckland Hospital into **Auckland Domain** (daily 24 hours; Wintergardens: Apr–Oct daily 9am–4.30pm, Nov–Mar Mon–Sat 9am–5.30pm, Sun 9am–7.30pm), New Zealand's oldest park and the site of a huge volcanic explosion that took place thousands of years ago. The wide crater has formed a natural amphitheatre arching from the hospital to the Auckland War Memorial Museum *(see p.28)* and is the venue of numerous outdoor sporting and cultural events. If you are arriving by taxi, ask the driver to point out the Wintergardens and Wintergardens Teahouse *(see p.29)* along the way. If you are on foot, head into the park from Park Road. If you are on the bus, get off on Parnell Road, slightly further southeast.

Food and Drink 🍴

② **WATERFRONT CAFÉ**
Maritime Museum Building, Viaduct Harbour; tel 09 359 9914; $
The Maritime Museum's café has a broad European-style menu and does great late breakfasts.

③ **REVIVE**
16 Fort Street; tel: 09 307 1586; $
Tasty, nutritious and affordable vegetarian fare, much of which is organic.

④ **VULCAN CAFÉ**
19 Vulcan Lane; tel: 09 377 9899; $$
The Vulcan Café is slap bang in the middle of this designer shopping area. Delicious Cajun chicken salad.

⑤ **FOODOO**
62 High Street; tel: 09 373 2340; $
Stylish delicatessen-style café with indoor and outdoor seating.

Above from far left: apartments by Viaduct Harbour; the view towards the Ferry Building.

Formal Gardens
The Auckland Domain's Formal Gardens evolved in the 1860s on a site on which the Auckland Acclimatisation Society tested and propagated exotic trees, birds and trout. Its duck ponds were the source, in 1866, of Auckland's first piped water supply.

All Blacks
Success in rugby is synonymous with New Zealand's All Blacks. For information on tickets to games, the history of the team and even the lowdown on the *haka* (the Maori dance performed prior to each game) visit www.allblacks.com.

Museum Library

Local Volcanoes

Auckland War Memorial Museum

The main sight in the park, the imposing **Auckland War Memorial Museum** ❼ (tel: 09 309 0443; www. aucklandmuseum.com; daily 10am–5pm; charge), enjoys a prime location with panoramic views of the Domain and parts of the city and harbour.

The museum was constructed in 1929 and provides an excellent overview of the natural, cultural and social history of New Zealand. For the first-time visitor it also provides a superb introduction to Maori culture through its collection of artefacts, including a raised storehouse, a carved meeting house and, possibly the most spectacular exhibit, *Te Toki a Tapiri*, a great Maori war canoe carved from a single totara log. This 25-m (82-ft) long boat was built in 1836 to seat approximately 100 warriors. There are daily performances featuring traditional Maori song and dance, and the 'Scars on the Heart' display depicts the compelling story of New Zealand at war.

As you walk around the museum, keep an eye out for Auckland's most revered volcanic peaks. These include: **One Tree Hill**, once topped by a lone summit pine but now marked only by an obelisk; **Mount Eden**; and the

Right: waterlilies in the Wintergardens.

slopes of **Rangitoto Island** *(see p.35)*. Note the names of locations etched in the stone around the entire museum façade: these were the battlefields where New Zealanders were killed in overseas wars in the 20th century.

The Wintergardens

There is a café in the museum, if you want a quick snack, but there's a treat in store if you walk from the front of the museum back down to the **Wintergardens Teahouse**, see ⑪⑥. On the south side of the teahouse, a take-away kiosk (daily 9am–5pm) sells ice creams and other snacks.

If time permits, take a stroll behind the tearooms through the **Wintergardens** ❽ (summer Mon–Sat 9am–5.30pm, Sun 9am–7.30pm; winter daily 9am–4.30pm; free), a conservatory housing some 10,000 exotic plants. Look out for the short native bush walk, which gives an indication of the type of vegetation still covering large tracts of the countryside.

PARNELL

From the Wintergardens, follow the path that runs south-east around the perimeter of the Domain and out to Parnell Road. Turn left here and take a 15-minute walk to **Parnell** ❾, a vibrant inner-city suburb known for its boutique shopping and wide range of eateries, such as **Trinity Café**, see ⑪⑦.

As you walk, look out, on your right, for **St Mary's Church** ❿ *(see margin, right)*, regarded as one of the finest wooden Gothic buildings in New

Zealand, and for the **Holy Trinity Cathedral** ⓫, which was completed only in 1995.

Just 30m (33yds) further, at the St Stephen's Avenue intersection, is a mix of bakeries, 'dairies' (small grocery stores), fish-and-chip shops and the start of the designer shops that become more apparent as you venture down the hill. Another good pitstop at this point is the **Strawberry Alarm Clock**, see ⑪⑧.

The Parnell Village complex on the left-hand side of Parnell Road comprises characterful wooden villas reclaimed and restored for retail purposes. Walk around the verandas and over the little bridges linking villa to villa to access the shops. For lunch and a chance to watch the world go by, get a seat under the awning at **Verve Café**, see ⑪⑨.

Above from far left: statues in the Wintergardens; the marina; smart town-houses in Parnell.

St Mary's Church
A church dedicated to St Mary has served Parnell parish since 1860. The present church was built between 1886 and 1897 on land opposite the cathedral. It was moved and rotated into its present position, with much controversy, in 1982.

Food and Drink

⑥ WINTERGARDENS TEAHOUSE
Auckland Domain; tel: 09 379 2020; $
A lovely setting for tea, with views over duck ponds and the meandering walkways of the Domain.

⑦ TRINITY CAFÉ
107 Parnell Road; tel: 09 300 3042; $
Sleek, tasteful and comfortable café, doing great breakfasts and brunches. A good spot to people-watch on the busy Parnell Road.

⑧ STRAWBERRY ALARM CLOCK
119 Parnell Road; tel: 09 377 6959; $
Just along from the Trinity Café, this is an unpretentious, laid-back venue, with an enticing range of paninis and brunch dishes.

⑨ VERVE CAFÉ
311 Parnell Road; tel: 09 379 2860; $$
The Verve Café is a relaxing spot with a nice decked area for alfresco dining/drinking. Classic café food.

Auckland University

The University of Auckland was formally opened on 23 May 1883 as Auckland University College, part of the University of New Zealand. A disused courthouse and jail served as premises for the 95 students and four teaching staff.

Today, the university is the largest in New Zealand, hosting over 40,000 students on five campuses.

Below: glass art.

BACK TO THE CENTRE

After pounding the pavements of Parnell, either hail a taxi or enjoy a half-hour walk back to the city centre. Your ultimate destination, on the corner of Federal and Victoria streets, is the landmark Sky Tower *(see p.32)*, which offers unparalleled views over the entire city, including its suburbs, the Waitakere Ranges and the islands of the gulf.

If you're on foot, veer left down Parnell Rise. Once at the bottom, walk under the rail bridge and cross the Grafton motorway extension, then take a deep breath before tackling the hill on the other side. A path leads from Churchill Road up through a reserve area to the junction of Symonds Street and Alten Road, to the Romanesque columns of the Presbyterian **St Andrew's Church**. Directly opposite the church is a low fence that surrounds the lower grounds of **Auckland University** *(see margin, left)*.

High Court

Cross over, head west along the Waterloo Quadrant and, on your right, you will see the old **High Court** ⑫, with its historic chamber and courtrooms joined to a modern extension. Work started on the old Court building in 1865, and the first sitting took place three years later. The carved stone heads and gargoyles adorning its exterior were crafted by Anton Teutenburg, a Prussian immigrant who was paid 15 shillings a day for the task.

Old Government House

Moving on, you will see, on the left-hand side, at 12 Princes Street, the **Old Government House** ⑬, completed in 1856 and the former residence of the Governor-General of New Zealand. Cross the road to the entrance and take a stroll through the grounds, now owned by Auckland University. The building appears to be stone but is in fact clad entirely in kauri, a tall coniferous tree that once dominated New Zealand's landscape. Walk alongside the building and enjoy the lush subtropical gardens on the hillside leading up to Princes Street.

Old Arts Building

Make your way up Princes Street, where on the left you will see the **Old Arts Building** ⓮, designed and built with the help of students from Auckland University College *(see margin left)* and opened in 1926. Locals call it the 'Wedding Cake', because of its ornate pinnacled white-stone construction.

Albert Park and Auckland Art Gallery

Opposite the Old Arts Building is **Albert Park** ⓯ (daily 24 hours), a beautifully maintained inner-city sanctum featuring a floral clock, statues of Queen Victoria and influential early colonial leader Sir George Grey (1812–98), a band rotunda and (usually) hordes of students lazing on the grass.

Now take one of the paths that lead downhill to Kitchener Street. On the corner of Wellesley Street is the **Auckland Art Gallery (Toi o Tamaki)** ⓰, heralded in 1888 as 'the first permanent art gallery in the Dominion'. Today, it is the largest art institution in the country, with a collection of over 12,500 works, including major holdings of New Zealand historic, modern and contemporary art, outstanding works by Maori and Pacific Island artists and European paintings, sculpture and prints from 1376 to the present.

It is divided into two galleries. The **Main Gallery** (tel: 09 379 1349; www.aucklandartgallery.govt.nz; daily 10am–5pm; free) displays mainly historical and European art collections, while the **New Gallery** ⓱ (corner of Wellesley and Lorne streets; tel: 09 379 1349; www.aucklandartgallery.govt.nz; daily 10am–5pm; free), which is accessed through a courtyard across the street, showcases cutting-edge contemporary art.

If you need refreshment at this point, **Jolt**, see ⑪⑩, is just to the west.

Above from far left: Parnell has great cafés for afternoon tea and cake; high-rise downtown Auckland; taking a break in Albert Park.

Below: tower of the Old Arts Building.

Food and Drink 🍴

⑩ JOLT

47 High Street; tel: 09 303 0066; $
This busy espresso bar is good for a pick-me-up, so ideal after perusing the collection at the Auckland Art Gallery. To reach it from the gallery, head north up Kitchener Street, west up Victoria Street, then right on to the High Street.

Above from left:
'sky-jumping' off
the Sky Tower;
dinghy in front of
the uninhabited
Rangitoto Island.

Auckland Markets
To get to the heart
of a city, find its
stomach. Nowhere is
Auckland's culinary
diversity more
apparent than at its
multicultural markets,
such as Otara market
in South Auckland
or the inner-west
Avondale market.
Here colourful
characters sell
exotic, inexpensive,
fresh produce.

SKY TOWER

To end your exploration of the city centre, walk one block down Queen Street in the direction of the sea. This leads to Victoria Street, where you should turn left and walk up the slope to Auckland's most prominent landmark, the **Sky Tower** ⓲ (tel: 09 363 6000; www.skytower.co.nz; daily 8.30am until late; charge for viewing deck only). At 328m (1,076ft) high, it is the tallest tower in the Southern Hemisphere, offering breathtaking views for more than 80km (50 miles) in every direction – weather permitting.

If the heartstopping elevator ride does not provide enough of an adrenalin rush, try the **Sky Jump** (Mission Control, Level 2, SKYCITY; tel: 0800 759 5867; www.skycityauckland.co.nz; daily 10am–6pm; charge), a wire-controlled 192-m (630-ft) leap from a platform near the viewing area.

SKYCITY

Adjacent is **SKYCITY** (tel: 09 363 6615; www.skycityauckland.co.nz; daily 24 hours), home to bars and entertainment areas. The ground-floor **Rebo Café & Bar** (daily 24 hours) has good views of the Sky Tower's 'sky-jumpers'.

Right: Maori art
and the Sky Tower.

AROUND AUCKLAND

Spend a couple of hours driving around Auckland's waterfront, then catch a ferry either to historic Devonport and, time permitting, to the uninhabited Rangitoto Island, or to verdant Waiheke Island.

Among Auckland's attractions are its Waitemata (meaning 'sparkling') Harbour and surrounding bays. Popular with watersports fans, they also provide the focal point for this tour.

ALONG TAMAKI DRIVE

This drive begins at the landmark **Ferry Building ❶** *(see p.26)* at 99 Quay Street, then continues east along Quay Street, with the port to your left. Shortly after you pass the container terminal (on your left), Quay Street becomes Tamaki Drive. Hobson Bay is on your left at this point, and **Parnell Baths** (tel: 09 373 3561; Mon–Fri 6am–8pm, Sat–Sun 8am–8pm; charge), an outdoor swimming complex, are on your right. Beyond, across the harbour, the most prominent feature is the volcanic cone of the uninhabited **Rangitoto Island** *(see p.35)*, an optional visit for later.

Continuing along Tamaki Drive, following the signposts to St Heliers, you will pass **Okahu Bay**, the first of a string of city beaches. On your right is the broad, grassy area of **Orakei Domain**.

KELLY TARLTON'S

As you drive around the bay, watch out on the right for a large building that houses Hammerheads seafood restaur-

DISTANCE 21km (13 miles), excluding the island tours
TIME A full day
START/END Ferry Building, Auckland
POINTS TO NOTE
You will need a car in order to follow this tour to the letter; for details of car-hire firms, *see p.111*. If you don't have a car, you could just follow the second part of the tour (ie the island visits). Remember to pack a bathing costume for the beach visits.

ant; use it as a landmark to move into the right-hand lane and turn into the car park at the well-signposted **Kelly Tarlton's Antarctic Encounter and Underwater World ❷** (23 Tamaki Drive; tel: 09 528 0603; www.kelly tarltons.co.nz; daily 9am–6pm; charge). There's lots to see, so plan to spend at least an hour and a half here.

When it was opened in 1985, this was the first aquarium of its kind in the world. Acrylic tunnels built under the sea take you through tanks of exotic New Zealand marine life. You can board a 'snow cat' to view penguins; the heated vehicles plunge through a 'white-out storm' to emerge in a recreated Antarctic landscape.

Above: on the beach; driving through a vineyard on Waiheke Island; baby penguin at Kelly Tarlton's.

Above from left:
olive trees and vineyard on Waiheke Island; sunrise over the Hauraki Gulf; bird's-eye view of Waiheke Island.

MISSION BAY

Resume your journey east for another 1km (½ mile) until you arrive at **Mission Bay ❸**. Turn left, off Tamaki Drive into either the first public car park or the second one near the large clock. Food-wise, there are lots of options, including **Riva**, see ⑪①, at the long line of eateries across the road from the beach. Alternatively, stock up on deli or bakery treats for a picnic on the lawn overlooking the beach; the spot by the fountain is a good choice for this. Afterwards, take a stroll along the promenade and perhaps take time out for a paddle.

Kohimarama and St Heliers

If you are feeling energetic, tackle the seaside walk to **Kohimarama ❹**, home to **Café on Kohi**, see ⑪②, 2km (1¼ miles) away, or to **St Heliers ❺**, a further 1km (½ mile), see ⑪③ and ⑪④. Every spring (usually March), this route is filled with tens of thousands of people on the 'Round the Bays' fun run. Check the date on www.roundthebays.co.nz, if you want to avoid this.

Ladies Bay and Achilles Point

To continue the drive, head up Cliff Road at the end of Tamaki Drive to **Ladies Bay** and the lookout at **Achilles Point ❻**. Note the plaque honouring HMS *Achilles*, which took part in the 1939 Battle of the River Plate, then retrace your path along Tamaki Drive to the Ferry Building.

ISLAND TOURS

There are two recommendations for the rest of the day: a trip to Devonport and, time permitting, Rangitoto Island, or a trip to Waiheke Island. For both, take the ferry, leaving your car on the Auckland side (Fullers ferries only carry foot passengers). Note that the last ferry from Devonport to Rangitoto leaves at 12.15pm. (It is also

Food and Drink

① RIVA
89 Tamaki Drive, Mission Bay; tel: 09 528 8566; $$
A class act serving modern European food on the main 'café row' of Mission Bay.

② CAFÉ ON KOHI
237 Tamaki Drive, Kohimarama; tel: 09 528 8335; $$
This relaxing spot on the beach does lovely coffee and nice lunches, and is a great place to enjoy a glass of wine at sunset.

③ ANNABELLES
409 Tamaki Drive, St Heliers; tel: 09 575 5239; $$
Friendly, efficient staff serve a wide variety of seafood.

④ KAHVE
1 St Heliers Bay Road, St Heliers; tel: 09 575 2919; $
Delicious Mediterranean-style fare served in an ambient, renovated 1920s store.

⑤ DEVONPORT STONE OVEN BAKERY AND CAFÉ
5 Clarence Street, Devonport; tel: 09 445 3185; closed Sun; $
Bakes 30 varieties of bread, all of which are fat-free and naturally fermented. Sourdough is a speciality. Good range of delicious cakes and pastries, plus excellent espressos.

⑥ STONYRIDGE
80 Onetangi Road, Waiheke Island; tel: 09 372 8822; $$
The Tuscan-style Stonyridge serves fine food and wine from its patios overlooking a north-facing valley of olive trees and grapevines. Advance booking advised.

⑦ MUDBRICK CAFÉ
Church Bay Road, Waiheke Island; tel: 09 372 9050; $$
The Mudbrick Café offers a winning combination of beautiful vineyard setting, varied menu, indoor and outdoor seating and great views of Auckland across the water.

possible to catch a ferry directly from Auckland to Rangitoto, but they only run at 9.15am and 10.30am, which makes them incompatible with the rest of this tour.)

Devonport and Rangitoto Island

Ferries for **Devonport** ❼ depart half-hourly from the Fullers Cruise Centre (Pier 1, Ferry Building, 99 Quay Street; tel: 09 367 9111; www.fullers.co.nz; daily 6am–11.30pm; charge); the crossing takes 12 minutes. Stroll up Victoria Street from the ferry terminal to the heart of the village. For information on sights, pop into the **Visitor Centre** (tel: 09 446 0677; Mon–Fri 8am–5pm, Sat–Sun 8.30am–5pm).

If the weather is good, consider hiking up the volcanic cones of **Mount Victoria** or **North Head** (check with the information centre for directions) for great harbour and gulf views, or visit Cheltenham Beach to relax and swim. Alternatively, browse Devonport's boutiques and antiques shops and relax at a café such as the **Devonport Stone Oven Bakery and Café**, see ⑪⑤.

If your timing is right, catch the 12.15pm ferry from Devonport to **Rangitoto Island** ❽ (the name means 'blood-red sky'). This 600-year-old volcano offers a mix of rugged lava outcrops and caves, lush native bush and sandy coves. Hike to the summit, which, at 260m (864ft), has spectacular views of Auckland and the Hauraki Gulf. Picnic beside the beach or hop aboard a four-wheel-drive volcanic explorer road train for a guided tour with Fullers (tel: 09 367 9111; www. fullers.co.nz; charge).

Waiheke Island

Another option is to visit **Waiheke Island** ❾ (ferries depart from Auckland's Ferry Building around every half-hour with Fullers; journey time: 40 minutes). Waiheke has beautiful beaches, vineyards, olive groves, native bush and laidback seaside villages. Options for exploring include hiring a mountain bike, purchasing a hop-on, hop-off bus pass, or joining a 1½-hour Explorer Tour or Vineyard Tour through Fullers (tel: 09 367 9111; www.fullers.co.nz). Alternatively, take it easy at **Stonyridge** or the **Mudbrick Café**, see ⑪⑥ and ⑪⑦.

Devonport's Three Mounts

Devonport is located at the tip of a sandy beach-fringed peninsula that protrudes into the Waitemata Harbour. Fabulous 360-degree views over Auckland, the Waitemata Harbour and the islands of the Hauraki Gulf can be enjoyed from any one of its three 'Mounts'. Of these, Mount Victoria Takarunga is just a short hike away from where the ferry drops passengers at the wharf.

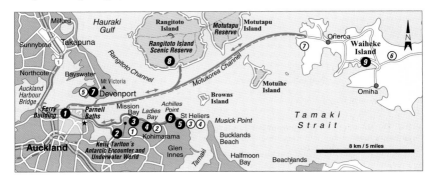

3

NORTHLAND

Kilometres of golden beaches, giant sand dunes, tranquil harbours, bush-clad islands and large tracts of ancient kauri forest are among the highlights on this driving tour of the North.

Scottish Links

Visitors to Waipu are greeted with signposts proclaiming in Celtic *Ceud Mile Failte* ('A hundred thousand welcomes'), reflecting the town's Scottish heritage: in the 1700s, some 900 hardy pioneers emigrated here. These links are celebrated at the annual Scottish games (country dancing and caber-tossing) on 1 and 2 January.

Above: tranquil fishing; thundering Whangarei Falls.

> **DISTANCE** 977km (607 miles)
> **TIME** Two to four days
> **START/END** Auckland
> **POINTS TO NOTE**
> You will need a car for this tour; for details of car-hire firms, *see p.111.* Note, however, that hire cars are not insured on Ninety Mile Beach. For details of hotels in this area, *see p.113.*

Northland is often called the 'birthplace of the nation', thought to have been the landing point of the Maori adventurer Kupe in the 10th century; it was home to New Zealand's first seat of government and was where the Treaty of Waitangi *(see p.39)* was signed in 1840.

Along Northland's eastern edge is the Bay of Islands, known for its picturesque 800-km (500-mile) coastline, which embraces around 150 islands. At the northern tip of the island is Cape Reinga, a place that is sacred to the Maori people *(see p.40).* On the West Coast attractions include Hokianga, a sheltered harbour with a score of ragged inlets, and the fine Ninety Mile Beach.

TOWARDS WHANGAREI

Leaving **Auckland ❶** early via SH1, cross the Auckland Harbour Bridge, then continue on SH1, following the signs to **Warkworth ❷**. For a breakfast stop, try **Bridge House Lodge**, see ⑪①, just under an hour from Auckland. Stretch your legs with a walk by the picturesque Mahurangi River.

Waipu and Whangarei

Driving another 100km (62 miles), past the small town of **Waipu ❸** *(see left;* also see ⑪②, if you need to stop) will bring you to Northland's main city (pop. 50,000) and erstwhile busy port, **Whangarei ❹**. As you enter on SH1, look out on the left for Tarewa Park, an information centre.

If time allows, take a sidetrip to the **Whangarei Falls**, which plunge 25m (82ft) into a tranquil, bush-fringed pool. Hike the 20-minute walk around the falls before rejoining SH1.

BAY OF ISLANDS

Kawakawa

Now follow the signs to **Kawakawa ❺** (about one hour from Whangarei), which is part of the Bay of Islands, a maritime park of around 150 islands and bays (more on this later – *see opposite*). Highlights in Kawakawa city centre include the public toilets, which were transformed in 1999 by the Austrian artist Friedensreich Hundertwasser *(see*

right). The toilets feature his trademark bright colours, organic forms and (most appropriate for this purpose) prolific use of tiles. For a meal in Kawakawa, try the **Trainspotters Café**, see ⑪③.

Paihia

At this point double back and turn off to **Paihia** ❻ via Opua. There is plenty to do in Paihia, a busy little town with lots of restaurants and hotels (see ⑪④ and ⑪⑤ and *p.113*); it is also the perfect departure point from which to explore the Bay of Islands. For more information, pop into the Bay of Islands Information Office (Maritime Building, Paihia Wharf; tel: 09 402 7683; www. northlandnz.com; daily 8am–5pm), a circular building on the wharf.

History abounds here: Captain Cook and his crew sheltered among these islands in 1769 and gave the area its name; New Zealand's first colonists settled in nearby **Russell**, and it became the first capital; and New Zealand's founding document, the Treaty of Waitangi, was signed here in 1840.

Getting out onto the water is very tempting, and there is a huge range of cruises and tours; reputable companies include Fullers Bay of Islands (Maritime Building, Paihia Wharf; tel: 09 402 7421; www.fboi.co.nz) and Kings Dolphin Cruises & Tours (Maritime Building, Paihia Wharf; tel: 0800 222 979; www.dolphincruises.co.nz), which between them offer a range of day and half-day trips, including the Cape Brett/Hole in the Rock voyage *(see right)*, the Original Cream (tall ship) Trip and swimming with the dolphins.

If time is short, we recommend prioritising the 'Hole in the Rock', the result of wind and sea erosion. For this, hop aboard the *Excitor* (Fullers, Maritime Building, Paihia Wharf; tel: 09 402 7421; www.fboi.co.nz) or *Mack-Attack* (Maritime Building, Paihia; tel: 0800 622 528; www.mackattack.co. nz), a 90-minute blast to the Hole in a powerful speedboat.

Russell

Most cruises offer the option of disembarking at **Russell** ❼. Set on a peninsula across the harbour, this quaint village is where New Zealand's first

Food and Drink

① BRIDGE HOUSE LODGE
16 Elizabeth Street; tel: 09 425 8351; $$
Next to the Mahurangi River, the Bridge House Lodge teams fresh produce with locally produced Matakana wines. There's a large patio area for summer dining and cosy fires in the winter.

② WAIPU CAFÉ & DELI
29 The Centre, Waipu; tel: 09 432 0990; closed Mon; $
Freshly prepared sandwiches, rolls and panini and decent coffee, served by friendly staff.

③ TRAINSPOTTERS CAFÉ
39 Gillies Street, Kawakawa; tel: 09 404 0361; $
Across the road from Hundertwasser's celebrated public loo, Trainspotters serves great coffee, cakes, snacks and light meals.

④ CAFÉ OVER THE BAY
Upstairs at The Mall, Marsden Road, Paihia; tel: 09 402 8147; $-$$
Enjoy a healthy menu and lots of vegetarian options from Paihia's Café over the Bay. As the name implies, the views are impressive.

⑤ CAFÉ NO.6
6 Marsden Road, Paihia; tel: 09 402 6797; $
This quaint, boutique-style café is perfect for a quick coffee or a light meal, and has ample outdoor seating with bay views.

Above from far left:
Northland beach;
carved Maori mask,
Waitangi National
Reserve; digging for
shellfish on North-
land's west coast;
fun on Te Paki
sand dunes.

On the Water

The essence of the
Bay of Islands cannot
be experienced
without getting out
on to the water.
Sports fishing is
legendary here;
famous American
game-fisherman Zane
Grey was based at
Otehei Bay in 1926
and dubbed it
'Anglers' Paradise'.
Charter a yacht or
board a traditional
creamboat (tall ship) to
cruise around this
paradise of 144
beautiful green islands
hemmed with biscuit-
coloured sands and
sheltered anchorages.
The more adventurous
can climb aboard a
powerboat for a
thrillingly fast excursion
to Piercy Island,
zipping through the
Hole in the Rock.

white colonialists settled. Local boat
companies also provide a ferry service
that crosses these waters every half-
hour (journey time: 15 mins). Book at
the Maritime Building or pay onboard.

Russell, once known as 'the hell hole
of the Pacific' and famous for its unruly
population of whalers and runaways, is
now a quiet town with a distinctly Victorian atmosphere. Walk along the
waterfront and seek out **Pompallier
House** (South End, The Strand; tel:
09 403 9015; www.historic.org.nz/
pompallier; daily, summer 10am–5pm,
winter 10am–4pm; charge), a Catholic
mission house dating to 1841, making
it the oldest survivor of its type in the
country. The gardens are particularly
attractive, and have fine views of the
Bay of Islands.

Also make time to visit the **Russell
Museum** (2 York Street; tel: 09 403
7701; www.russellmuseum.org.nz;
daily 10am–4pm; charge), which documents the development of the town
from its early days as a Maori village to
the present day. Highlights of the collection include a model of Captain
Cook's ship *Endeavour*. Other activities in Russell include hiking up
Flagstaff Hill, where Maori warrior
Hone Heke and his men felled the
British flagpole four times.

Take a break from your sightseeing
at one of the many fine eateries lining
the waterfront. The **Duke of Marlborough**, see ⑪⑥, is a good choice for
food and is also an option if you want
to stay the night in Russell. For other
hotel recommendations, *see p.113.*

Haruru Falls

At this point, return to Paihia, as there
are a couple of sights nearby well worth
visiting. The first is **Haruru Falls** ❽,
once the location of New Zealand's first
river port. To reach the falls drive 3km
(2 miles) down Puketona Road, or,
if you're feeling adventurous, explore
this waterway by kayak with Coastal
Kayakers (Te Karuwha Parade, Ti Bay,
Waitangi; tel: 09 402 8105; www.
coastalkayakers.co.nz).

Waitangi Treaty House

After viewing the falls, retrace your
route and then follow the signs to the
Waitangi National Reserve ❾ (tel: 09
402 7437; www.waitangi.net.nz; daily
9am–5pm; charge). Allow at least
an hour to stroll the grounds and view

Food and Drink 🍴

**⑥ DUKE OF
MARLBOROUGH**

35 The Strand, Russell; tel: 09 403
7829; www.theduke.co.nz; $$–$$$
The menu at the restaurant in this
smart waterfront boutique hotel has
French foundations, but the New
Zealand influences are strong. Local
oysters and mussels are brought
straight from the sea to the table, and
the Northland beef is commendable.

⑦ POSH NOSH

3 Homestead Road, Kerikeri; tel:
09 407 7213; closed Sun; $
Posh Nosh does Mediterranean cuisine with a stress on Spanish dishes.
Try their divine gazpacho made using
freshly picked sun-ripened Kerikeri
tomatoes. The breakfast menu is
wide-ranging European fare and
comes with freshly roasted coffee.

the **Whare Runanga** (Maori meeting house), which depicts the ancestors of many Maori tribes in its intricate carvings, *waka* (Maori war canoe) and the **Waitangi Treaty House**, where New Zealand's founding document was signed in 1840. Have lunch at the contemporary Waikokopu Café, located in the Treaty House grounds, or return in the evening for a recommended cultural production performed by local Maori (tel: 09 402 5990; www.culturenorth.co.nz; charge).

TOWARDS CAPE REINGA

At this point you can either return to Auckland via SH1 on the route already travelled, return via the West Coast's SH12, or travel north for another 223km (140 miles) to **Cape Reinga**. Note that the round trip to Cape Reinga can also be completed as a day's drive from Paihia. Alternatively, a number of operators, including Fullers (Maritime Building, Paihia Wharf; tel: 09 402 7421; www.fboi.co.nz), run coach and four-wheel-drive tours from Paihia. Most drive one way via the beach highway of Ninety Mile Beach *(see p.40)* and return by road.

Kerikeri

For those driving themselves north, breakfast is best enjoyed in the vibrant township of **Kerikeri ❿**, a haven for the gourmet traveller with locally produced wine, olives and avocadoes, cheese, ice cream and chocolate; **Posh Nosh**, see ⑪⑦, is our recommendation for refreshment.

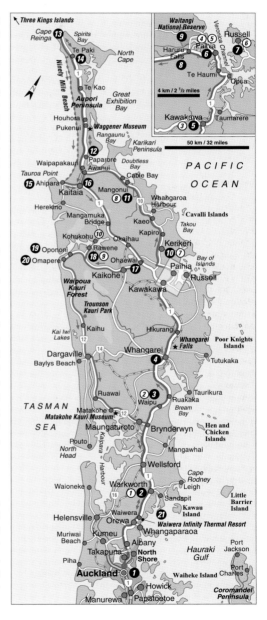

Maori Tradition
According to Maori traditions, the spirits of the departed leap from an 800-year-old pohutukawa tree on the windswept Cape Reinga to begin the voyage back to their final resting place in the ancestral homeland of Hawaiki.

Before you leave town visit the historic **Kemp House** (246 Kerikeri Road, Kerikeri Basin; tel: 09 407 9236; www.historic.org.nz; daily: summer 10am–5pm, winter 10am–4pm; charge), New Zealand's oldest-standing European building, erected in 1822 by the Reverend Gare Butler as a mission house. Also look out for the adjacent **Stone Store** (times as above), built in 1832 to house food for the mission.

Mangonui, Awanui and Paparore

Continue north on SH10 through the fishing village of **Mangonui** ⑪, home to New Zealand's best fish-and-chip shop, see ⑪⑧, and on to **Awanui**, rejoining SH1. At Awanui, the **Ancient Kauri Kingdom** (229 SH1, Awanui; tel: 09 406 7172; www.ancientkauri.co.nz; daily 9am–5pm; free), where 30,000–50,000-year-old swamp kauri logs are crafted into a range of furniture and housewares, is worth a look.

Nearby, in **Paparore** ⑫, the **Gumdiggers Park** (171 Heath Road; tel: 09 406 7166; charge) offers an insight into the old gumdigging days – when settlers dug for kauri gum, used to make varnish – at its 100-year-old gumfield.

Cape Reinga

Rejoin the northbound SH1 to **Cape Reinga** ⑬. This is a place of great spiritual significance to Maori people, who believe it is 'the place of the leaping', where the souls of the dead gather before they enter the next world *(see left)*. Weather permitting, the **Three Kings Islands**, named by Abel Tasman in 1643, will be visible on the horizon, while the spectacular Cape Maria Van Diemen dominates the west. To the east the long curve of Spirits Bay leads the eye to the North Cape.

THE WEST COAST

Ninety Mile Beach

The icing on the cake of a trip to the cape involves driving one way along the magnificent sandy highway of **Ninety Mile Beach**, entering or exiting on **Te Paki Stream** ⑭. Note, however, that this is only possible if you are in a non-hire vehicle, as the latter are not insured on the beach. (If you are in a hire car, simply head south instead on SH1.) If the Ninety Mile Beach trip is an option for you, consider also hiring a sand toboggan through a local tour operator to slide down the vast **Te Paki Dunes**; continue on to the beach's magnificent unbroken arch of white sand to **Ahipara** ⑮, at the southern tip.

Food and Drink 🍴

⑧ MANGONUI FISH AND CHIP SHOP
Beach Road, Mangonui; tel: 09 406 0478; $
This fish-and-chip shop overhangs the Mangonui Harbour and serves fresh, locally caught fish (watch as it is unloaded at the wharf). Succulent Blue nose, served with lemon, is the speciality.

⑨ THE BOATSHED CAFÉ
8 Clendon Esplanade, Rawene; tel: 09 405 7728; $
Situated in a renovated shed on stilts overhanging the harbour, this café does fresh New Zealand fare. From the terrace watch the mist rising from mangroves as water laps beneath your seat.

⑩ WATERLINE CAFÉ
2 Beach Road, Kohukohu; tel: 09 405 5552; $
A short ferry ride across the Hokianga Harbour leads to the Waterline Café, which – like the Boatshed, *above* – is built on stilts over the harbour. Highly recommended paninis.

BACK TO AUCKLAND

To return to Paihia at this point, travel via **Kaitaia** ⑯ and **Kawakawa** on SH1. To return to Auckland from Paihia via the West Coast, turn off SH1 on to SH12 at **Ohaeawai** ⑰. For your first glimpse of the Hokianga Harbour, take the turn off to **Rawene** ⑱, a picturesque harbourside town on the peninsula. Noteworthy buildings here include **Clendon House** (8 Clendon Esplanade; tel 09 405 7874; www.historic. org.nz; summer Mon–Sat 10am–4pm, winter Mon–Tue 10am–4pm; charge), an 1860s building that was home to James Reddy Clendon, an early trader and member of the first Legislative Council from 1844. Displays in the house give insight into early colonial life.

A good stopping point here is the **Boatshed Café**, see ⑨⑨, where you can relax and watch the changing tide and the comings and goings of the vehicular ferry that transports locals and visitors across to **Kohukohu**. If you decide to take the ferry, another option for a bite to eat is the **Waterline Café**, see ⑨⑩, on the Kohukohu side.

Opononi

Back on SH12, a 19-km (12-mile) drive leads to **Opononi** ⑲, the largest town of the Hokianga, and one-time home of Opo, a young, friendly bottle-nosed dolphin who adopted the town and played with children in the summer of 1955–6. Morning, afternoon and evening harbour cruises are run daily by Crossings Hokianga (29 SH12, Opononi; tel: 09 405 8207;

crossingshokianga.com), as are sport fishing and sand tobogganing on the vast dunes at the harbour's entrance.

Omapere and Waipoua Forest

The small town of **Omapere** ⑳ (known for its lake) provides a last glimpse of the Hokianga Harbour before you enter the **Waipoua Forest** on SH12. The forest is home to the massive kauri tree and an ideal place to wander in the type of dense vegetation that once cloaked New Zealand. There are several walks to enjoy here, the most popular being the five-minute stroll to see the 2,000-year-old Tane Mahuta, the largest kauri of all.

Kai Iwi Lakes and Baylys Beach

Heading south on SH12, other popular attractions include the **Kai Iwi Lakes** and the pounding shores of **Baylys Beach**, before you reach the flats of **Dargaville** and **Ruawai**, lush with kumara (sweet potato) crops.

Be sure to stop near Matahoke at the **Matakohe Kauri Museum** (tel: 09 431 7417; www.kauri-museum.com; May–Oct 9am–5pm, Nov–Apr 8.30am–5.30pm; charge) and lose yourself for a while in bygone days of kauri-felling, gumdigging and hardy pioneers, before rejoining SH1 to Auckland.

Waiwera Thermal Resort

Consider stopping en route at the **Waiwera Infinity Thermal Resort** ㉑ (21 Main Road, Waiwera; tel: 09 427 8800; www.waiwera.co.nz; daily 9.30am–10pm; charge), where you can relax in the waters of its hot thermal pools before returning to the bustle of the city.

Above from far left: west coast beach; cycling along Ninety Mile Beach; visitors dwarfed by the trunk of Tane Mahuta, in Waipoua Forest.

Above: sleepy cat at Kemp House; the Stone Store.

COROMANDEL PENINSULA

This two-day driving tour leads from the old gold-mining township of Coromandel, across the ranges to Mercury Bay's magnificent Cathedral Cove, then south to the resort area of Pauanui and Tairua.

Firth of Thames

The Firth of Thames shelters an abundance of birdlife, and provides some of New Zealand's best driving, winding through tiny beachside settlements, interspersed with cliffs gripped by ages-old red-blossoming pohutukawa. Along the route, take time to wander through Rapaura Water Gardens; stop in at Tararu's exotic Tropical Butterfly and Orchid Garden; and enjoy an ice cream on the beach.

DISTANCE 452km (281 miles)

TIME Two days

START Auckland

END Auckland or Tauranga

POINTS TO NOTE

You will need a car for this tour; for details of car-hire firms, *see p.111*. Take care as you approach the Kopu Bridge, which spans the Waihou River. It is a long one-lane bridge controlled by traffic lights, so make sure you wait until the lights are green. We recommend a mining tour in Thames, so take sensible footwear with closed toes with you. Aim to arrive at Hot Water Beach *(see p.45)* for low tide, if you can.

(see p.111) ... *(see p.45)*

Food and Drink 🍴

① SOLA CAFÉ

720 Pollen Street, Thames; tel: 07 868 8781; $

In the heart of the Grahamstown area of Thames (to the north of the centre), this vegetarian café serves generous portions, and has a wheat- and gluten-free menu. While you indulge in nutritious fare such as layered eggplant-and-polenta lasagne, you can check out the work of local artisans decorating the café walls.

The rugged Coromandel region is one of New Zealand's most ruggedly beautiful, with waterfalls, secluded hot springs, huge expanses of windswept beach festooned with driftwood, and old gold mines. In the 19th century, the peninsula was exploited for kauri timber, kauri gum (used in varnishes) and gold. Stands of forest were axed, but some remain, providing a home for rare species of frog, the North Island crow (korako), hundreds of kingfishers and seabird colonies (on offshore islands). Semi-precious stones such as carnelian, agate, chalcedony and jasper are washed down from the hills into creeks to mingle with the pebbles on the western beaches.

Auckland to Thames

Thames, the gateway to the Coromandel Peninsula, is a straightforward 90-minute drive from **Auckland ①**. Start on Queen Street and drive up to Karangahape Road; turn left, then veer right before Grafton Bridge, following the signs to SH1. Follow SH1 south for about 20km (12½ miles) and just after the Bombay take the turn-off for SH2, signposted to Tauranga. Follow the highway another 50km (31 miles) before you turn east on to

SH25, signposted to Thames. The road heads out across the low-lying former swamplands of the Hauraki Plains. Over 1,000km (620 miles) of drains and canals have turned this land into productive dairy pasture, though it is still prone to occasional flooding. Cross the Kopu Bridge *(see grey box, left)*, which spans the Waihou River, and you will reach a T-junction at the base of the Coromandel Range. Turn left and drive 5km (3 miles), following the signs to Thames.

THAMES

Nowadays, **Thames ❷** (pop. 7,000) is predominately a service town for the outlying rural communities, but in the second half of the 19th century, it had the largest population in New Zealand, with around 18,000 inhabitants and well over 100 hotels – due to its goldmines.

Make your first stop the **Tourist Information Centre** – the teal-green building on the right as you enter the town (206 Pollen Street; tel: 07 868 7284; www.thames-info.co.nz; Mon–Fri 8.30am–5pm, Sat–Sun 9am–4pm). Here, you can pick up brochures and information on activities in the region.

Drive down Pollen Street, the town's main thoroughfare, for glimpses of its heyday. Some of the old buildings of the mining era remain, notably the renovated **Brian Boru Hotel** *(see p.114)*, at the corner of Richmond and Pollen streets. This is a good place, if you want to stay overnight, and is also pleasant for a drink at the end of the day. The **Sola Café**, see ⓜ①, is also on Pollen Street, if you need refreshment.

Mining Town

To continue the tour, follow Pollen Street north and turn right back on

Above from far left: kayaking around Cathedral Cove; coastal cliffs; sunbather looking out to sea; kiwi lookout post.

Coromandel Forest Park

Behind Thames is the Coromandel Forest Park, with 50km (31 miles) of well-maintained hiking tracks to explore.

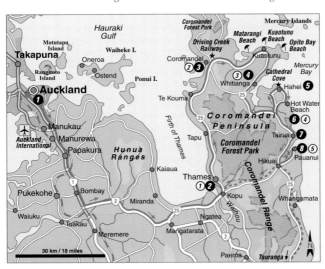

**Fishy Treats
in Coromandel**
Be sure to sample
local green-lipped
mussels or catch
a fish and have it
smoked at the
Coromandel Smoking
Company (70 Tiki
Road, Coromandel;
tel: 07 866 87 93;
www.corosmoke.co.
nz) before you
leave town.

SH25, then quickly right again for the **Goldmine Experience** (corner of SH25 and Moanataiari Road; tel: 07 868 8514; www.goldmine-experience. co.nz; daily 10am–4pm; charge).

The original site of the 1868 Gold Crown claim now features a photographic exhibition of Thames. The well-informed hosts will take you on a tour of an old mine shaft; the tour, which takes at least 40 minutes, can be muddy during the wetter months, so go prepared with closed-toe footwear. For those who dislike being in confined dark spaces, there are alternative activities here, including gold-panning.

COROMANDEL TOWNSHIP

Continue north on SH25, travelling along the waterline on a route lined with pohutukawa trees (red-blossoming New Zealand Christmas trees) that grow so thickly that the telephone lines have to leave the bank and journey across the water instead, to **Coromandel ❸**. Take a walk around the town, which has an arty atmosphere, to admire its Victorian buildings and relics from the gold-mining and timber industries. For a bite to eat, visit **Pepper Tree**, see ⑪②, on Kapanga Road, in the centre.

Head north, up Kapanga, Rings, Colville and Buffalo roads to soak up local history. First, try your hand at gold-panning and admire the waterwheel at the **Coromandel Stamper Battery** (410 Buffalo Road; tel: 07 866 7933; daily in summer 10am–5pm; charge). Return to the main road, then turn right onto Driving Creek Road for

the **Driving Creek Railway** (380 Driving Creek Road, Coromandel; tel: 07 866 8703; www.drivingcreekrailway. co.nz; daily 10am–5pm; charge), a 27-year-old project still evolving under the direction of Barry Brickell, one of the country's most respected potters. A narrow-gauge 15-inch track, with tunnels, spirals and a double-decker viaduct, zigzags uphill past sculptures to the 'Eyeful Tower', a wooden terminus with gorgeous views of the peninsula.

WHITIANGA

After your exploration of Coromandel township, resume your drive, crossing the Coromandel Range on SH25. En route to Whitianga, visit the beautiful East Coast beaches of Matarangi, Kuaotunu and Opito Bay.

Whitianga ❹ is the main hub for marine-based activities departing for the **Te Whanganui A Hei Marine Reserve**, which stretches from Cooks Bluff and Motukoruro Island through to Mahurangi Island. Charter boats such as *Escapade* (tel: 07 866 8703; www.islandcruise.co.nz; charge) offer fishing trips, charter cruises, kayaking and diving. Pitstops here include **Zest Café**, see ⑪③, in the centre of town.

HAHEI

Make time to visit the village of **Hahei ❺**, 16km (10 miles) south. Here, you can rent a kayak for a guided trip to the stunning **Cathedral Cove**, where a gigantic arched cavern penetrates the headland, with Cathedral Cove

Kayaking (88 Hahei Beach Road; tel: 07 866 3877; www. seakayak tours. co.nz; daily; charge) or hop aboard the *Hahei Explorer* (62 Hahei Beach Road; tel: 07 866 3910; www.dreamland.co. nz/haheiexplorer; daily 10am and 2pm; charge). Cathedral Cove can also be reached on foot, on a track that leads down from a lookout point above the Hahei.

HOT WATER BEACH

To soak in your own freshly dug pool at **Hot Water Beach** ⑥, drive south 10km (6 miles) and turn off, following the signs to Hot Water Beach. Aim to arrive around low tide (your accommodation hosts or Visitor Information Centre will be able to advise you on tide times). Hire a spade for $5 from **Hot Waves Café**, see ⑪④, or borrow one from your accommodation, and stroll north along the beach. A rocky outcrop marks where you can dig holes in the sand. Wallow in the hot-spring waters until the tide begins to turn.

Note that it is not safe to swim at Hot Water Beach, owing to strong currents.

TAIRUA AND PAUANUI

Further south on SH25 is the town/ resort of **Tairua** ⑦. The very best views of its harbour and white beach can be had from the top of Mount Paku – Maori legend has it that if you climb to the peak of the mountain you'll return within seven years; the outstanding views may entice you to do this anyway.

The neighbouring community of **Pauanui** ⑧ is a popular playground for wealthy Aucklanders and a great place to relax. Popular local activities include swimming, surfing, fishing, diving, bush walks and golf. **Miha Restaurant**, see ⑪⑤, is right by the beach.

BACK TO AUCKLAND

From here, you can return to your base in Auckland via SH25A, which travels through the Coromandel Forest Park to Kopu, where you can retrace your steps to Auckland. Alternatively, you can link this tour to the next one *(see p.46)* and continue on to Tauranga. To do so, drive 34km (21 miles) south on SH25 to the summer beach resort of **Whangamata**, after which it is an easy 100-km (62-mile) journey through the gold-mining township of Waihi and on to SH2 to Tauranga.

Whangamata
In Whangamata, beach life reigns, and surfers rule; fishing is immensely popular, and even swimming with dolphins is not an infrequent occurrence. With two good golf courses, mountain biking in the forest and walking trails including the Wharekirauponga, Wentworth Valley and Luck at Last Mine tracks, there are lots of landbased activities to enjoy too.

Food and Drink

② PEPPER TREE
31 Kapanga Road, Coromandel Township; tel: 07 866 8211; $$
Serves light, fresh New Zealand cuisine at breakfast, lunch and dinner. Space for indoor and outdoor dining.

③ ZEST CAFÉ
5 Albert Street, Whitianga; tel: 07 866 4833; $$
For a small town, Whitianga has quite a few cafés. Zest is one of the most popular, with its tasty fusion menu and excellent cakes.

④ HOT WAVES CAFÉ
8 Pye Place, Hot Water Beach; 07 866 3887; $–$$
Hot Waves serves delicious home-made food in an ambient cottage. Tables spill into a large native bush garden.

⑤ MIHA RESTAURANT
Mount Avenue, Pauanui Beach; tel: 07 864 8088; $$$
Pacific Rim flavours blended with a modern European twist.

5 TAURANGA DISTRICT

This driving tour of the Tauranga District in the Bay of Plenty can begin from Rotorua, travelling through the kiwifruit-growing area of Te Puke to Mount Maunganui, or in reverse in conjunction with tour 4 (see p.42).

Kiwi-Farming
The fertile soils and warm climate of the Bay of Plenty nurture the vines that produce 80 percent of the country's kiwifruit behind tall windbreaks.

Below: Mount Maunganui and Tauranga Harbour.

> **DISTANCE** 166km (103 miles)
> **TIME** A full day
> **START/END** Rotorua
> **POINTS TO NOTE**
> A car is needed for this journey; for car-hire firms, *see p.111*. Allow about 90 minutes for the direct return journey from Rotorua to Tauranga. Bring a swimming costume, if you want to bathe at the spa at the end of the tour.

The Tauranga District is an easy day trip from Rotorua, 86km (53 miles) along an attractive northbound route. It is part of the Bay of Plenty, an area that Maori travelled vast distances in a series of migrations over several hundred years to make their home. Since then, the relaxed settlements along this coastline have continued to draw visitors from far and wide.

TOWARDS OKERE FALLS

In **Rotorua ❶**, start at the **i-SITE Visitor Information Centre** on Fenton Street. Turn left and follow SH30 out of town, travelling past Te Ngae and the airport, and continuing straight ahead on SH33 to Okawa Bay and Lake Rotoiti. Make **Okere Falls ❷**, at the head of Lake Rotoiti, your first stop of the day. Take the sharp left turn just past the Okere Falls shop and follow the signs to a small car park. This is the start point of an easy 10-

> **Food and Drink** 🍴
> ① **KIWI 360 CAFE**
> SH2, Te Puke; tel: 573 6340; $
> Enjoy lunch on a covered balcony overlooking the vines. The excellent menu includes seafood, salads, posh pizzas and freshly baked cakes, including own-recipe kiwifruit muffin.

minute walk along the Kaituna River to a lookout point. If you're feeling adventurous you can whitewater raft its 7-m (23-ft) falls, the highest commercially rafted waterfall in the world, with Raftabout (Okere Falls Bridge, SH33; tel: 07 343 9500; www.raftabout.co.nz; daily 9am, noon, 3pm).

TE PUKE

Continuing for about 25km (15½ miles) by car from Okere Falls, watch for signs to **Longridge Park ❸** (316 SH33, Paengaroa; tel: 0800 867 386; www.longridgepark.co.nz; daily 9am–5pm; charge). Here, daredevils can hop aboard a thrilling jet-boat ride or whitewater raft the lower reaches of the Kaituna River.

Kiwi 360

Shortly after Longridge, the road meets SH2. Make a left turn here towards the fertile soils of **Te Puke,** New Zealand's major kiwifruit-growing area. Just past the turn-off to Whakatane you will see a sculpture of the giant kiwifruit that marks **Kiwi 360 ❹** (35 Young Road, Te Puke; tel: 07 573 6340; www.kiwifruitcountry. co.nz; daily 9am–5pm; charge); this working kiwifruit farm offers informative rides through the orchards aboard a comfortable cart train. The café here, see ⑪①, is a popular choice for lunch.

MOUNT MAUNGANUI

A roundabout 16km (10 miles) beyond Te Puke signals the approach of Tauranga and **Mount Maunganui ❺**. Do

not veer left on SH2, but continue on what becomes Maunganui Road. Follow it about 4km (2½ miles) to reach what locals dub 'The Mount'. This refers to the town's namesake, Maunganui, a conical rocky headland that rises to a height of 232m (761ft) above sea level and was one of the largest early Maori settlements in New Zealand.

The well-signposted **i-SITE Visitor Centre** (Salisbury Avenue; tel: 07 575 5099; www.nztauranga.com) can provide guides to hikes on the mountain.

Follow Salisbury Avenue round past the sheltered **Pilot Bay** to the base of the mount, park near the Domain

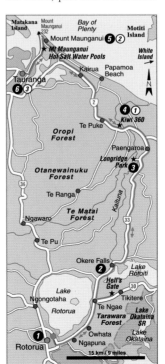

Above from far left: disused wharf pillars in Tauranga Harbour; the view from Mount Maunganui over Tauranga; the unmistakable giant kiwifruit, marking Kiwi 360.

Up the Mountain
The extinct volcanic cone of Mount Maunganui rises above a safe, sheltered inner-harbour beach. The walkway that leads to the mountain's summit is dotted with seats offering amazing harbour, ocean and city views.

Above from left:
shady trail leading up
Mount Maunganui;
gondola ride over
Rotorua; having a
crazy time Zorbing.

White Island
In the southern Bay
of Plenty is the lunar
landscape of White
Island, where jagged
red ridges rise around
yellow and copper
fumeroles, discharging
gas so pressurised it
roars like a squadron
of B52 bombers.
Despite the formidable
terrain, the island has
incredible allure,
mainly since this is the
only place in the world
where you can see an
active marine volcano
at such close prox-
imity. For further
information, contact
Pee Jay Tours
(15 The Strand East,
Whakatane; tel: 07
308 9588; www.
whiteisland.co.nz).

campgrounds, then follow signs to the
start of the tracks. Depending on how
energetic you feel, you can either take
the Summit Road Track to the top of
the mountain, or enjoy a stroll on the
circular track around the base.

Have a picnic on the beach at Pilot
Bay or head to Marine Parade to tackle
the surf on the sweeping white sands
of Mount Maunganui Beach. Inexpensive food can be purchased from any of
the tearooms and cafés that line Maunganui Road, behind Mount Drury
Reserve (and within easy walking
distance of both beaches); **Café Hasa
Baba**, see ①②, is our recommendation.

TAURANGA

After lunch make your way to **Tauranga**
❻, driving back along Maunganui
Road and cutting a sharp right at the
roundabout to head along SH29
(Hewletts Road) and over the harbour
bridge. As you come off the bridge,
follow the signs left at the roundabout
to the city centre and park your car on
The Strand near the railway station.
Stroll to the north end of **Herries Park**
and cross the road to see the ceremonial canoe, *Te Awanui*, on display.

A path at the base of the hill takes
you through the pleasant **Robbins
Park** and **Rose Garden** to the **Mon-
mouth Military Redoubt**. British
troops were stationed here during
unrest in the 1860s, and their earth-
works and guns survive as reminders of
the bloody conflict between Maori and
Pakeha in days gone by.

Back on The Strand, a short walk
brings you to the main shopping
precinct and Devonport Road, where
you can enjoy afternoon tea at a local
café such as **Mediterraneo**, see ①③,
before retracing your steps to Rotorua.

Pools and Spas
On the way back, stop at the **Mount
Maunganui Hot Salt Water Pools**
(Adams Avenue; tel: 07 575 0868; www.
hotpools.leisurecentre.co.nz; Mon–
Sat 6am–10pm and Sun 8am–10pm;
charge) for a refreshing swim, or a
communal mud spa overlooking the
thermal reserve at **Hell's Gate** (tel: 07
345 3151; www.hellsgate.co.nz; daily
8.30am–8.30pm; charge), in Tikitere.

To get to the pools, turn off SH33
at Te Ngae on to SH30 and travel
4km (2½ miles), parking right outside
the complex. Take a stroll around the
thermal park, where highlights include
an accessible mud volcano and the
beautiful **Kakahi Falls**, the largest hot
waterfall in the Southern Hemisphere,
before succumbing to the mud spa.

This is a gloriously relaxing place,
where you can cake yourself with detoxi-
fying mud, then soak in a hot thermal
pool. Go private at the adjoining (more
expensive) Wai Ora Spa.

Food and Drink 🍴

② CAFÉ HASA BABA
16 Pacific Avenue, Mount Maunganui; tel: 07 574 8200; $
Middle Eastern café serving superb mezze and moussaka.

③ MEDITERRANEO
62 Devonport Road, Tauranga; tel: 07 577 0487; $
Serves the best coffee in town, plus a tasty all-day breakfast, a
blackboard menu, and deli-style salads, pastries and sandwiches.

ROTORUA

Set amid crater lakes, Rotorua offers stunning scenery in an active volcanic wonderland of spouting geysers, bubbling mud pools, fumaroles and natural thermal springs. This driving tour covers its highlights.

Rotorua, as the locals proudly boast, is the only place in New Zealand where you can tell exactly where you are with your eyes closed. They are referring, of course, to the distinctive aroma of sulphur that permeates the town, courtesy of its boiling mud pools and hot springs. To visit Rotorua with your eyes shut would be a travesty, however, because it is an area of rich cultural and scenic beauty. Block your nose and head out boldly; you will soon become accustomed to the smell.

The town (pop. 64,500) was a popular tourist destination in the 1800s, when visitors came to marvel at the naturally formed Pink and White Terraces *(see p.52)*. Today, it is one of the jewels of New Zealand tourism, a place of thermal wonders, lush forests, green pastures and (usually) crystal-clear lakes abounding with fighting trout. No fewer than 10 lakes are now the playground of anglers, campers, swimmers, waterskiers, yachtsmen and hunters.

Rotorua is also a major centre for Maori culture – one third of the city's population is Maori. Marae (tribal meeting-places) dot the area.

GONDOLA RIDE

Aim to leave around 9am to ensure you don't miss the 10.30am farm show

DISTANCE 33km (20 miles)
TIME At least a full day
START/END Rotorua
POINTS TO NOTE
A car is needed for this journey; for car-hire firms, *see p.111.* Bring a swimming costume if you want to bathe at the Polynesian Spa.

at Rainbow Farm and Springs later on in the tour *(see p.50)*. Head west on Arawa Street, then turn right on to Ranolf Street (the start of SH5). This drive takes you past **Kuirau Park** on your left, a 25-ha (62-acre) reserve. Drive on, and along Fairy Springs Road about 4.5km (3 miles) out of the city, and turn into the car park at **Skyline Skyrides Gondola ❶** (tel: 07 347 0027; www.skylineskyrides.co.nz; daily 9am–late; charge); there's a café here, see Ⓨ①, if you would like refreshment. Within minutes of buying a ticket you will be whisked sharply up the 900-m (2,953-ft)

Thrills and Spills
Rotorua is the place to dive out of your comfort zone into any number of crazy thrills. A good place to begin is at the Agrodome in Ngongotaha (Western Road, Ngongotaha; tel: 07 357 1050; www.agrodome. co.nz; charge), 6km (4 miles) from city centre. Climb into a Zorb, a big, fat, clear-plastic ball, and roll full tilt downhill, protected from serious harm by an air cushion. If that's not wacky enough, you can kit up in a flying suit, goggles and gloves, and levitate spreadeagled in mid-air above a 150-km/h (93-mph) blast of jet stream rushing from a 900-hp twin-turbo DC3 aircraft propeller.

Food and Drink
① TERRACES CAFÉ
Fairy Springs Road; tel: 07 347 0027; $
Terraces Café has a broad menu, ranging from the all-day breakfast to freshly made sandwiches and cakes, fish and chips, gourmet pizzas (the house speciality) to sushi. Fantastic views.

Kuirau Park

Thermal parks abound in Rotorua, and most have an entry fee, but at Kuirau Park, at the junction of Ranolf Street and Lake Road to the west of the city centre, you can stroll in off the street and see plopping mud and steam billowing from fumeroles to your heart's content, before visiting its aquarium and sending the kids (if you have them) for a fun ride on a miniature railway.

slopes of Mount Ngongotaha for glorious views of the region that you will soon be exploring.

On the return journey, ride back down on the gondola or take the luge, a three-wheel cart, on the exciting 1-km (³/₄-mile) long downhill track.

RAINBOW FARM AND SPRINGS

A further 100m (110yds) along Fairy Springs Road are **Rainbow Farm and Springs ❷** (tel: 07 347 9301; www. rainbownz.co.nz; daily 8am–9pm; charge), on your right and left respectively. Park by the springs and follow the signs leading you under the road

to the farm. Every day at 10.30am (also at 11.45am, 1, 2.30 and 4pm), a show introduces visitors to New Zealand's farming heritage. Strapping farm lads take you through the finer points of mustering and shearing sheep, and a range of other farm activities.

After strolling around the farm, take the path back under the road to Rainbow Springs, showcasing more than 150 species of native New Zealand fauna set among freshwater springs and pools filled with rainbow and brown trout. There's a nice café here: **The Springs Café**, see ⑪②. Allow one to two hours for the whole experience.

AROUND LAKE ROTORUA

Return to your car and follow SH5 back towards town, turning off on to Lake Road. Stop at the lakefront parking area near the jetty, where every day at 12.30pm the *Lakeland Queen* (tel: 0800 572 784; www.lakeland queen.co.nz; charge), a 22-m (72-ft) paddle steamer takes passengers around **Lake Rotorua** from the **Lakeland Queen Launch Jetty ❸** on a lunchtime cruise. (Note that breakfast and dinner cruises are also available.)

While dining you will be regaled with the love story of Hinemoa and - Tutanekai, a Maori legend similar to *Romeo and Juliet*, but with a happier ending. (If you miss the boat, you can eat at the **Lakeside Café**, see ⑪③.)

Ohinemutu

There's plenty to see around the lake, so after lunch take a stroll northwest of the

---

Food and Drink

② THE SPRINGS CAFÉ
Fairy Springs Road; tel: 07 350 04440; $
This place does a filling 'Big Breakie' panini, sandwiches, scones and cakes. Lovely setting by the café's own vegetable patch.

③ LAKESIDE CAFÉ AND CRAFTS SHOP
Memorial Drive; tel: 07 349 2626; $$
If you miss the boat, or choose not to sail, 50m (55yds) to your left (facing the lake) is the Lakeside Café and Crafts Shop, where you can have lunch and browse through a selection of works by local artisans.

④ THE THAI RESTAURANT
1147 Tutanekai Street; tel: 07 348 6677; $
Authentic country-style Thai cuisine with robust flavours.

⑤ FAT DOG CAFÉ
1161 Arawa Street; tel: 07 347 7586; $
Cheerful, cosy, laid-back place that does big servings of basic hearty New Zealand classics. One for dog lovers, with canine-themed decor and a clientele of pampered-pooch owners.

⑥ RELISH CAFÉ
1149 Tutanekai Street; tel: 07 343 9195; $$
Fashionable café serving fresh, innovative Kiwi fare.

café along the narrow driveway that heads past the **Rotorua Yacht Club** and along the waterfront to **St Faith's Church** and **Ohinemutu** ❹. This tiny lakefront village was the main settlement here when Europeans arrived in the 1800s. Today it's renowned for its idyllic little church, built in 1885, with its beautiful stained-glass window, an etched window depicting a Maori Christ figure who looks as though he is walking on the waters of Lake Rotorua, and a bust of Queen Victoria. The church was presented to the Maori people of Rotorua in appreciation of their loyalty to the Crown and is an impressive expression of how the Maori adopted Christianity into their traditional culture.

Tutanekai Street

Leaving the lakefront, take **Tutanekai Street**, Rotorua's main drag, where you will find a wide variety of shops, including a vast number of souvenir stores and dining options including **The Thai Restaurant**, **The Fat Dog** and **Relish Café**, see ⓴④–⑥.

Museum of Art and History

Now head east on Arawa Street and Queen Drive and past the Convention Centre and into the Government Gardens. Within its grounds is the **Rotorua Museum of Art and History** ❺ (Queens Drive; tel: 07 349 4350; www.rotoruamuseum.co.nz; summer daily 9am–8pm, winter daily 9am–5pm; charge). The 1908 Tudor-style building showcases art exhibitions and displays of slightly sinister-looking

apparatus used for hydrotherapy more than a century ago. Permanent exhibitions tell the story of the local Te Arawa people and the devastating eruption of Mount Tarawera in 1886.

WHAKAREWAREWA

It's now time to practise pronouncing the name of your next destination, **Whakarewarewa** ❻ (far-car-rear-wah-rear-wah), the closest thermal resort to the city. To reach it, head on to Fenton

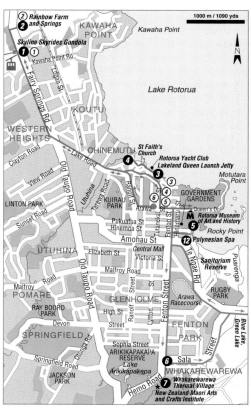

Above from left:
mud, glorious mud;
spectacular views of
the Tarawera Crater; a
restorative face pack.

Street – home to the town's Visitor Information Office (1167 Fenton Street; tel: 07 348 5179; www.rotorua nz.com; daily 8am–5.30pm, till 6pm in summer) and turn left.

After driving down Fenton Street for 3km (2 miles), you will see on your left the **New Zealand Maori Arts and Crafts Institute** (SH30; tel: 07 348 9047; www.nzmaori.co.nz; daily 8am–5pm; charge), where you can watch Maori carvers and flax weavers at work. Beside this is Whakarewarewa, which has extensive thermal activity, ranging from bubbling mud pools and boiling

springs to the famous Pohutu Geyser, which erupts up to 30m (98ft) high.

Allow at least 90 minutes to explore this area and the adjacent **Whakare-warewa Thermal Village** ❼ (17 Tryon Street; tel: 07 349 3463; www.whakare warewa.com; daily 8.30am–5pm; charge). You can take a guided tour and meet the Tuhourangi/Ngati Wahiao people who live among the geothermal activity and make use of the energy garnered from hot springs and steam vents for cooking purposes, as well as the natural mineral waters used for communal bathing.

BLUE AND GREEN LAKES

From Whakarewarewa, it's a scenic 20-minute drive to the Blue and Green Lakes. Head back up Fenton Street towards town and turn right into Sala Street; follow the street out to Te Ngae Road (SH30) and then turn off on Tarawera Road, the first main road to your right. Approximately 10km (6 miles) from the city, along the forest-fringed Tarawera Road, you suddenly drop down to opalescent **Lake Tikitapu**, otherwise known as the **Blue Lake** ❽.

Weather permitting, this is a great place for a swim; alternatively you can hike around its shoreline or hire a canoe or pedal boat from the Blue Lake Holiday Park across the road.

Continuing on, the road rises to a crest, from which you can see Lake Tikitapu and the larger **Lake Rotokakahi**, or **Green Lake** ❾, resting side by side. The waters of the Green Lake are *tapu*

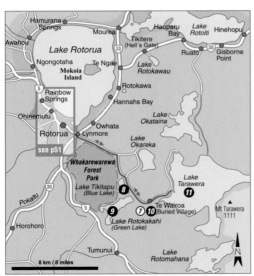

Food and Drink
❼ BURIED VILLAGE CAFÉ
Tarawera Road; tel: 07 362 8287; $
The café within the Buried Village does tasty home-cooked fare such as cakes, biscuits, slices, freshly filled rolls and hot savouries.

(sacred) to local Maori, and are not open for watersports.

PINK AND WHITE TERRACES

The road continues along an historic tourist route opened in the 19th century to the former **Pink and White Terraces**, once known here as the eighth wonder of the world. The naturally formed silica terraces on the shores of Lake Rotomahana were like a giant staircase, with a fan-shaped edge spilling across almost 300m (328yds) of lakefront. But nature proved unkind to its own wonders, and on 10 June 1886 a massive volcanic eruption of Mount Tarawera obliterated the terraces and buried two Maori villages beneath layers of ash and mud.

Te Wairoa

A memorial to the tragedy is located just a few minutes' drive past the Green Lake – the **Buried Village ⑩** excavation of Te Wairoa (1180 Tarawera Road; tel: 07 362 8287; www. buriedvillage.co.nz; daily: summer 9am–5.30pm, winter 9am–4.30pm; charge). Parking is available in front of the Buried Village souvenir shop and café, see ⑪⑦.

A marked walk takes you through the village excavations and sites, including its Maori *whare* (house), a flour mill, blacksmith's shop, a store and a hotel. Take in the village's eerie atmosphere in the shade of poplar and sycamore trees, a legacy of the early European settlers – and keep an eye out for the *whare* in which a Maori elder, who had foretold the tragedy, was trapped for four days before being rescued alive.

Depending on time and energy levels, you can either make your way past an animal enclosure back to the entrance to the Buried Village, or take the longer, but highly recommended, bush track that crosses Te Wairoa stream and leads steeply down through dense native bush to a waterfall and rapids. Continue on this route and you'll arrive back at the souvenir shops and café.

LAKE TARAWERA

From the Buried Village, Tarawera Road continues to **Lake Tarawera ⑪**, where a lookout point provides good views of the looming hulk of Mount Tarawera across the lake. Head downhill to the waterfront and Tarawera Landing, which is located on a quiet pumice-fringed bay with a small jetty. If your timing is right, take a scenic lake cruise (tel: 07 362 8595; departs daily between 9am and 4pm; charge).

SPA DELIGHTS

There's no better way to end a day in Rotorua than a soak in thermally heated water. Retrace the route back to Fenton Street and turn right into Hinemoa Street to the lakeside **Polynesian Spa ⑫** (Lake End, Hinemoa Street; tel: 07 348 1328; www.polynesianspa.co.nz; daily 8am–11pm; charge). Here you can enjoy a relaxing dip in restorative geothermal waters and perhaps treat yourself to a therapeutic massage.

Tamaki Maori Village
Time permitting, top off this busy day with a pre-booked Maori *hangi* and cultural show at the Tamaki Maori Village (SH5; tel: 07 349 2999; www. maoriculture.co.nz; daily; charge). You'll be collected from your accommodation and taken on a 20-minute bus journey to a replica village in an atmospheric forest. Local guides introduce Maori culture, myths and legends, song and dance, and then there's the opportunity to experience a *hangi*, a traditional method of steam-cooking food in an earth oven on top of red-hot stones. At the close of ceremonies, you can end the evening with a *hongi* – a traditional pressing of noses to signify friendship.

TAUPO

This driving tour is an easy day trip from Rotorua, heading south to Orakei Korako, then on to Huka Falls and Lake Taupo, New Zealand's largest lake. Stay another day and drive the volcanic loop around the mountainous Tongariro National Park, possibly en route to Wellington.

DISTANCE 96km (59 miles), excluding Tongariro National Park; 343km (213 miles) including the park
TIME One to two days
START Rotorua
END Rotorua or Wellington
POINTS TO NOTE
You will need a car for this tour; for details of car-hire firms, see p.111. Book in advance for any therapeutic treatments you might want at Taupo Hot Springs (see p.57).

Above from far left: still morning on Lake Taupo; jet boat on the Waikato River.

Below: Huka Falls.

New Zealand's largest lake, Lake Taupo, is fed by sparkling ice-melt from the mountains of the Tongariro National Park. It was formed by volcanic activity – an eruption so large that it was recorded by Chinese and Roman writers. The region's extraordinary landscape and unique range of cultural experiences make it a 'must-see' on any New Zealand itinerary.

The township of Taupo is situated on the shores of Lake Taupo, about 90km (56 miles) south of Rotorua. From the i-SITE Visitor Information Office on Fenton Street in **Rotorua** ❶, follow this road south past **Whakarewarewa** on to SH5.

THERMAL WONDERLAND

If you're looking to do a day tour, you will need to choose one option from the following three thermal parks listed; however, if you plan to stay overnight in Taupo there will be time to fit in at least two options.

Waimangu Volcanic Valley
About 20km (12½ miles) south of Rotorua on SH5 you will pass the turn-off to **Waimangu Volcanic Valley** ❷ (587 Waimangu Road; tel: 07 366 6137; www.waimangu.com;

daily 8.30am–5pm; charge), a hotbed of thermal activity unearthed by the 1886 eruption of Mount Tarawera. Attractions here include the volcanic area around Waimangu Cauldron, the Inferno Crater and Ruamoko's Throat, typified by craters, volcanic lakes and hot springs. A walk through the valley, returning by shuttle bus, takes about one to two hours.

Wai-o-Tapu

Back on to SH5 and 10km (6 miles) further south you will pass the turn-off for the **Wai-o-Tapu Thermal Wonderland** ❸ (Loop Road; tel: 0800 768 678; www.geyserland.co.nz; daily 8.30am–5pm; charge). This sight is famous for the **Lady Knox Geyser**, which (with a little human assistance – soap is poured onto the geyser to release the surface tension) blows its top at 10.15am each day, and the boiling Champagne Pool, which flows over green silicate terraces. Allow at least an hour to explore.

Lake Ohakuri

Closer to Taupo (22km/13½ miles past the turn-off to Atiamuri) look for the signposts leading to **Orakei Korako** ❹ (494 Orakei Korako Road; tel: 07 378 3131; www.orakeikorako. co.nz; daily 8am–4pm; charge) on the shores of **Lake Ohakuri**. A boat waits to ferry travellers to a pristine geothermal field surrounded by unique silica terraces. Encompassing 35 active geysers, plopping mud pools and fizzing hot springs, this park also features an extremely rare geothermal cave. Allow an hour to explore.

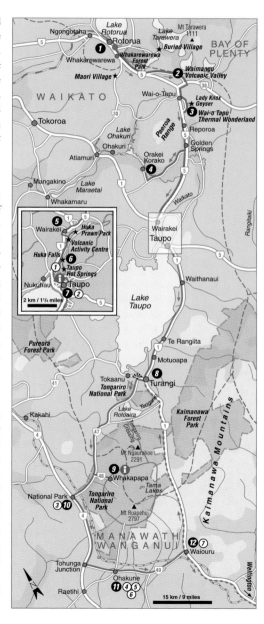

Taupo Watersports

Lake Taupo regularly plays host to international watersports events and is popular with residents and visitors alike for sailing, kayaking, windsurfing and numerous other sports and activities.

Below: serious business at the Huka Prawn Park.

WAIRAKEI PARK

Continue driving: only 2km (1¼ miles) before **Wairakei ❺**, SH5 joins with SH1. Just past Wairakei, on your left, look for the turn-off to the **Volcanic Activity Centre** (Wairakei Park; tel: 07 374 8370; www.volcanoes.co.nz; Mon–Fri 9am–5pm, Sat–Sun 10am–4pm; charge), which has informative displays on the region's geography.

Huka Prawn Park

Other interesting activities on this section of the Waikato River include the world's only geothermal prawn farm, the **Huka Prawn Park** (Wairakei Park, Taupo; tel: 07 374 8474; www.prawnpark.co.nz; daily 9am–4.30pm; charge), where you can feast on juicy tropical prawns while enjoying views of the river as it begins its 425-km (264-mile) journey to the sea.

Honey Hive

Also in the park is the **Honey Hive** (Wairakei Park; tel: 07 374 8553; www.

honeyhivetaupo.com; daily 9am–5pm; free), the country's largest honey centre, selling honey-scented soaps, lotions and wine. There's also honey-tasting, a picnic area and a ride for children.

Jet-Boat Ride

Leaving here, follow the signs from the car park for a thrilling spin on the Waikato River with Huka Jet boat rides (Wairakei Park; tel: 07 374 8572; www.hukajet.co.nz; daily 10am–5pm, departures every half-hour). This adrenalin-pumping ride is guaranteed to leave you breathless.

HUKA FALLS

The most stunning feature in this area are the thundering **Huka Falls ❻**. To reach them, turn left and follow the signs 2km (1¼ miles) to the Huka Falls car park. A short walk takes you to views of the falls, where up to 270 cubic metres (9,535 cubic ft) of water are tumultuously pushed through a long, narrow gorge before plunging into a deep pool. There are several good walks in the area, including the four-hour return journey along the river to the Aratiatia Rapids.

Pitstops on the Huka Falls Road include the **Huka Vineyard Restaurant**, see ①.

TAUPO

From here it's a short car ride through to **Taupo ❼**. Make a stop at the signposted lookout on the left just heading into town; it provides panoramic views of the lake and mountains of the Ton-

gariro National Park. This vast expanse may seem serene, but don't be fooled; over the past 27,000 years this crater has erupted 28 times. Hot springs and spas are testimony to the fact that this region has not yet run out of steam.

Follow SH1 from here into Taupo township. The Taupo **i-SITE Visitor Centre** (Tongariro Street, Taupo; tel: 07 376 0027; www.laketauponz.com; daily 8.30am–5pm) is easy to find on your right as you enter the town. If you want to pick up brochures from here, continue a little past it to the lakefront, turn right into the lakeside car park, then walk back.

Lake Taupo

No follow the road down to the wharf and marina, where various cruises depart across on **Lake Taupo** throughout the day. Highly recommended is a trip on the *Ernest Kemp*, a replica 1920s steamer, which leaves daily at 10.30am and 2pm, with an extra sailing at 5pm from Jan–Oct (tel: 07 378 3444; charge).

Alternatively, hop aboard a catamaran tour with Chris Jolly (tel: 0800 252 628; www.chrisjolly.co.nz; daily 10.30am and 2pm; charge) and cruise around Acacia Bay and Rangatira Point, bound for Whakaipo Bay, where a display of contemporary Maori rock carvings can be seen on a cliff face. These were commissioned by the Queen Elizabeth Arts Council in 1980 and created by artists of the local Tuwharetoa tribe.

If you would like refreshment at this point, walk north up Tongariro Street and take the third right, Horomatangi Street; **Villinos**, see ①②, is at no.47.

Bungy-Jumping and Hot Springs

Those with energy to burn may want to wait until later for lunch and instead enjoy a bungy-jump over the **Waikato River** with **Taupo Bungy** (202 Spa Road, Taupo; tel: 0800 888 408; www. taupobungy.co.nz; daily 8.30am–5pm; charge). Just beyond the jump site is a parking area. It's an easy walk from the lower car park down to the river's edge, where you can paddle in a natural hot spring that mixes with cold river water.

Alternatively, soak in thermal pools ranging from 37 to 41ºC (99–106ºF), at **Taupo Hot Springs** (Napier-Taupo Highway; tel: 07 377 6502; www.taupo hotsprings.com; daily 7.30am–9.30pm; charge), followed by a therapeutic massage. Booking is essential.

Food and Drink

① HUKA VINEYARD RESTAURANT

56 Huka Falls Road, Taupo; tel: 07 377 2326; $$$
Taupo's only winery restaurant serves up mouthwatering cuisine in an exquisite setting of landscaped gardens and pinot noir vines. Enjoy one of the chef's signature platters while seated on the expansive patio with panoramic views of Mount Tauhara and surrounds. Sample wine at the cellar door adjacent to the restaurant.

② VILLINOS

47 Horomatangi Street, Taupo; tel: 07 377 4478; $$–$$$
This is the place to enjoy a bowl of scrumptious, steaming seafood chowder teamed with freshly baked ciabatta bread. A great haunt by night, Villinos is also perfect for celebrating a special occasion and good for a civilised lunch (open from 11.30am).

Above from far left: Tongariro's barren volcanic landscape, which served as Mordor in the *Lord of the Rings* movies, is punctuated by vividly coloured lakes and lava formations; the mountain in winter.

Lake Taupo
Lake Taupo last erupted 1,800 years ago; its average depth is 110m (360ft); its length is 46km (25 nautical miles); its width is 33km (18 nautical miles); and its total area is 616 sq km (238 sq miles). During winter the lake averages 11ºC (52ºF) and in summer 18ºC (64ºF). The lake is known for its fabulous trout fishing, but in New Zealand it is illegal to buy or sell trout, so if you wish to dine on this delicacy you must catch your own. Enquire at the i-SITE Visitor Centre, where staff will match you up with an experienced local skipper or guide. Skilled fly-fisherfolk will enjoy the wilderness experience of Taupo's wealth of local rivers, but bear in mind that river fishing operates purely on a catch-and-release basis.

Above from left:
skiing at Whakapapa;
natural steam bath;
mountain fun.

Ski Country
In winter, the Whaka-
papa Ski Field, 8km
(5 miles) from Whaka-
papa Village, teems
with snowboarders
and skiers of all
abilities. Huge, snow-
filled basins with steep
chutes, drop-offs and
powder stashes
provide an ample
playground for all; a
variety of lessons is
available. Turoa Ski
Field, on the other
side of the mountain,
has a wide-open bowl
that faces southwest
and offers good
conditions in October
and November.

If you are doing this tour as a day
tour, retrace your steps at this point
to take you back to Rotorua. If you
want to continue the tour, stay
overnight in Taupo *(see p.114)*, then
follow on as described below.

VOLCANIC LOOP

The first stop on the second day of this
tour is Tongariro National Park, which
offers blue and emerald lakes, waterfalls,
rocky plateaux, twisted thickets of native
bush, huge open landscapes and snowy
slopes, and can easily be explored from
Taupo or en route to Wellington.

Turangi
Head out of Taupo on SH1 and drive
to **Turangi** ❽, a village on the banks
of the Tongariro River. Turangi is the
place to rediscover the thrill of angling
or to take a ride aboard a whitewater

raft with **Tongariro River Rafting** (tel:
0800 101 024; www.trr.co.nz; departures daily: summer 9am and 2pm,
winter noon; charge).

Tongariro National Park
Leaving Turangi on SH47, make a stop
at the lookout on the right-hand side
before continuing the ascent through
dense forest into **Tongariro National
Park**. Beneath Mount Tongariro, with
its red craters, is **Lake Rotoaira** and the
Opotaka Historic Reserve (free).

After passing the reserve, you'll see
brown, windswept plains of toitoi,
manuka and flax, then the charred
cinder cone of **Mount Ngauruhoe**,
which last erupted in 1975. Man-
gatepopo Road provides access to the
Tongariro Crossing, New Zealand's
best one-day hike *(see box, below left)*.

The majestic snowy crown of **Mount
Ruapehu** dominates the route (SH48)
to **Whakapapa Village** ❾, a small ski
village with a range of accommodation
and cafés. The Visitor Centre provides
information on local hikes, including
the Mount Ruapehu summit walk,
Taranaki Falls and Tama Lakes.

At this point, if the budget allows,
take a scenic flight with Mountain Air
(corner of SH47/48; tel: 0800 922 812;
www.mountainair.co.nz; daily 8am–
5pm). Alternatively, continue on to the
township of **National Park**, ❿ a home
from home for snow junkies in the
winter ski season, with a climbing wall,
equipment hire and numerous cosy
bars and cafés (such as the **Railway
Station Café**, see ❨⫟❩③), at the junction of SH47 and SH4.

Tongariro Crossing

The 17-km (10½-mile) Tongariro Crossing, New Zealand's best
one-day hike, passes the steep, charred sides of Ngauruhoe,
the mineral-stained walls and active fumeroles of Tongariro's Red
Crater, and the vivid Emerald Lakes, contrasting sharply with
the burnt earth hues of the surrounding lunar-like landscape.
Further on is the gleaming Blue Lake, also known as Te Rangi-
hiroa's Mirror, after the son of
a chief who explored the
region in AD 1750. The views
are spectacular. The hike finishes on SH46, and transport
to and from the track can be
organised at all local hotels.

Ohakune

Follow SH4 south to Tohunga Junction, then turn off onto SH49 to **Ohakune** , a fast-growing après-ski hub offering easy access to the Turoa ski slopes up the picturesque mountain road dense with mountain beech forest, dwarf shrubs, and alpine flowers and shrubs. Lunch spots here include the **Alpine Restaurant**, **Altitude 585** and **Utopia Café**, see ⑪④–⑥.

Waiouru

From Ohakune, SH49 continues on to rejoin SH1 at **Waiouru** ⑫, home to the NZ Army's largest training camp and the **Army Memorial Museum** (SH1, Waiouru; tel: 06 387 6911; daily 9am–4.30pm; charge), where a sensitively curated collection of army memorabilia captivates military enthusiasts and civilians alike. The museum café, **Rations**, see ⑪⑦, is a good place for a break.

END OF TOUR

From here, you can choose to return to Taupo via SH1, travelling through the dry, desolate landscape of the Rangipo 'desert', before retracing your route back to Rotorua; alternatively, continue south towards Wellington. The 370-km (236-mile) journey on SH1 takes around five hours from Taupo, or 261km (162 miles) and four hours from Waiouru, and travels through Taihape, Bulls, Levin, and then down the Kapiti Coast to Wellington.

Tangiwai Tragedy
Proof of the region's volatile geology can be seen at the Tangiwai rail disaster memorial, on SH49 between Ohakune and Waiouru. Here, in 1953, a lahar flooded the Whangaehu River, destroying the Tangiwai Railway Bridge and killing 153 people. Fortunately, when Mount Ruapehu's Crater Lake burst its banks again, in March 2007, an alarm system provided a warning, before a torrent of mud and debris poured through the river gorge.

Food and Drink

③ RAILWAY STATION CAFÉ
National Park Railway Station, National Park; tel: 07 892 2881; $–$$
Housed inside the once-to-be-demolished, now renovated National Park Railway Station building, this atmospheric café is a great place to hang out. The food is fresh and home-made.

④ ALPINE RESTAURANT
Corner of Clyde and Miro streets, Ohakune; tel: 06 385 9183; $$
This smart restaurant does European-style cuisine. The atmosphere is warm and welcoming.

⑤ ALTITUDE 585
79 Clyde Street, Ohakune; tel: 06 385 9292; $
The ever-popular Altitude 584 offers hearty, reasonably priced pub fare, from curry to fish dishes.

⑥ UTOPIA CAFÉ
47 Clyde Street, Ohakune; tel: 06 385 9120; $
Great coffee, all-day breakfasts, delicious café fare (tasty paninis) and an extensive wine list. Open fire in winter.

⑦ RATIONS CAFÉ
SH1, Waiouru; tel: 06 387 6911; $.
This popular café, housed in Waiouru's Army Memorial Museum, is reputed to serve New Zealand's best breakfast – the SAS English breakfast, which comes piled high from 9am to 2pm. The main lunch menu here is also good, with the likes of 'Gallipoli Pot-pie', gourmet Cajun chicken sandwiches, pasta dishes and curries that change daily.

WELLINGTON

Vibrant Wellington, the seat of government and the unofficial cultural centre of the country, has a cosmopolitan buzz. This full-day walking tour explores its many highlights.

What's in a Name?

The earliest name for Wellington, from Maori legend, is Te Upoko o te Ika a Maui. This means 'the head of Maui's fish'. Caught and pulled to the surface by Polynesian navigator Maui, the fish became the North Island. Evidence of early Maori settlement and cultivation can be found at sites all across the Wellington Peninsula.

Wellington has an assurance and an international flair that comes with being the country's artistic and cultural heart as well as its capital city. With a regional population of about 440,000, including about 200,000 in the city itself, Wellington is considerably smaller than its northern rival, Auckland, which it replaced as capital in 1865.

Recent Development

Although a quiet, unassuming place until the late 20th century, in the last couple of decades New Zealand's capital has blossomed into a vibrant, urban destination with a lively nightlife. The city's charm derives partly from its quirky topography, with wooden turn-of-the century houses clinging to steep hillsides bristling with native bush and clumps of arum lilies. Zigzag streets spill downwards to the heart of the city,

the harbour and the affluent promenade of Oriental Bay. The layout reminds some visitors of San Francisco.

Wellington is nicknamed the 'Windy City', and that's no exaggeration; it's usually breezy, and at times the wind can knock you clean off your feet. In the business district, old higgledy-piggledy Wellington has virtually been replaced by soaring modern buildings – a cause of regret for many who loved the haphazard character of the old layout.

MUSEUM OF NEW ZEALAND

The tour starts at the **Museum of New Zealand – Te Papa Tongarewa ❶** (Cable Street; tel: 04 381 7000; www.tepapa.govt.nz; Fri–Wed 10am–6pm, Thur 10am–9pm; free), the city's star attraction. It has a vast collection, incorporating interactive displays, virtual-reality games and special exhibitions (many of which change frequently), so pick up a map in the foyer first to make the most of your time here.

Highlights

The museum's highlights include the permanent exhibition of Maori myths and legends of creation, a simulated earthquake, displays of bones of the extinct giant moa (a flightless, wing-

less bird, hunted into extinction in the 16th century) and a swing-bridge walk through a section of recreated native bush.

CITY CENTRE

To see more of the city, head north out of Te Papa, following the waterline towards the city's commercial centre. Watch out for in-line skaters as you make your way past the rowing clubs by **Frank Kitts Park**. Situated across the road is the city's vast **Civic Square** ❷, home to the **Michael Fowler Centre** (a concert and conference hall), the Edwardian-style **Town Hall** and the **Wellington City Library**, a gorgeous plaster curve of a building, decorated with metal palms. Tucked away between these civic buildings is the Art Deco **City Gallery** (tel: 04 801 3021; www.citygallery.org.nz; daily 10am–5pm; free), known for its con-

Above from far left: bird's-eye view of Wellington's harbour; hotel on Lambton Quay, one of the city's main thoroughfares.

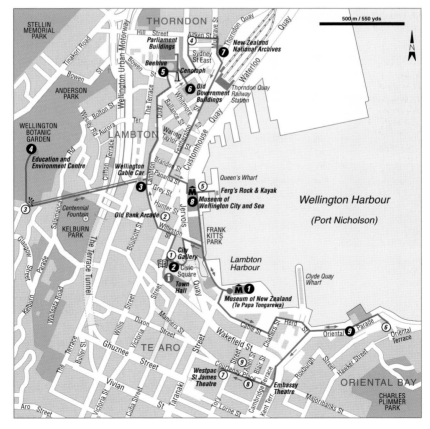

Above from left: sign for Museum of New Zealand – Te Papa Tongarewa *(see p.60)*; cable car to Upland Road and the Botanic Garden; the Beehive.

temporary art exhibitions (and home to the **Nikau Gallery Café**, see ⑪①), and the **Wellington i-SITE Visitor Centre** (tel: 04 802 4860; www. wellingtonnz.com; daily 9am–6pm).

Lambton Quay

After picking up more information on the city, head west, leaving the square via the archway next to the library. Cross Victoria Street and walk one more block to Willeston Street. Turn left and now you are on **Lambton Quay**, the heart of the city's commercial and retail area. Banks, accountancy and law firms vie with shop owners here and on **The Terrace**, a block behind, for some of the country's most expensive retail space.

If you're wondering why it's called a quay, when there's none in sight, the answer is that there was one on this site 150 years ago, before an earthquake in the 1850s reclaimed some more land for the city. Browse the shops and take a stroll through the stunning Victorian **Old Bank Arcade**, diagonally opposite the State Insurance Tower. Combine boutique shopping with a refreshment break at **Caffè Astoria**, see ⑪②.

New Zealand Designers
Wellington's shopping scene is second to none. Designer names to look out for include Karen Walker, Zambesi *(catwalk show illustrated above, bottom)* and local Wellingtonians Mandatory, Starfish, Voon and Andrea Moore.

Wellington Cable Car

About 150m (164yds) up Lambton Quay you will see the sign for the **Wellington Cable Car** ❸ (Lambton Quay; tel: 0800 801 700; Mon–Fri 7am–10pm, Sat 9am–10pm, Sun 10.30am–10pm; charge). Cars leave every 10 minutes from Lambton Quay and take you effortlessly up a steep incline, under the motorway and over Kelburn Park to Upland Road for

splendid views over the city and harbour. A good choice for lunch is the **Skyline Café**, see ⑪③.

BOTANIC GARDEN

If the weather is good, take a stroll after lunch around the adjacent **Wellington Botanic Garden** ❹ (daily dawn–dusk; free), 25ha (62 acres) of protected native forest, conifers, specialised plant collections and floral displays. It is classified as a Garden of National Significance by the Royal New Zealand Institute of Horticulture and is an Historic Places Trust Heritage Area.

Wander off the main paths to appreciate the gardens fully, but ultimately aim for the **Education and Environment Centre** (Mon–Fri 9am–4pm, Sat–Sun 10am–4pm), where you can learn about New Zealand's flora from a variety of interesting displays.

Afterwards, return to the cable car for the ride back to Lambton Quay.

THE BEEHIVE

After disembarking the cable car, turn left back on to Lambton Quay and walk to the end where it meets Bowen Street. Cross over and you are at the circular **Beehive** ❺, the seat of political power in New Zealand. Designed by the British architect Sir Basil Spence and constructed between 1969 and 1980, it houses the executive wing of Parliament, including the office of the Prime Minister. Walk past the **Cenotaph**, through the gates, and follow the sweeping drive up to the Beehive and

the adjacent **Parliament Buildings**, dating to 1922.

Make your way to the **Visitor Centre** (tel: 04 471 9503; Mon–Fri 10am–4pm, Sat 10am–3pm and Sun noon–3pm; free) in the foyer for an informative 45-minute guided tour that runs on the hour. The tour provides insight into how the building was 'earthquake-proofed' during its last renovation.

Old Government Buildings
Also of interest here are the **Old Government Buildings** ❻, set opposite the Cenotaph on Lambton Quay. Claimed to be the largest wooden building in the Southern Hemisphere, it was erected in 1876 using over 9,290sq m (100,000sq ft) of timber.

If you're thirsty, head 50m (55yds) up Molesworth Street, which runs in front of the Parliament grounds, to the **Backbencher** pub and café, see ⑪④.

NATIONAL ARCHIVES

From the Backbencher, walk down Aitken Street to Mulgrave Street. Across the road are the **National Archives** ❼ (10 Mulgrave Street; tel: 04 499 5595; www.archives.govt.nz; Mon–Fri 9am–5pm; Sat 9am–1pm; free), where you can view New Zealand's national records, including the nation's founding document, the Treaty of Waitangi.

QUEEN'S WHARF AREA

From the National Archives building, head back into town along Mulgrave Street; walk past Thorndon Quay

Railway Station, then continue straight along Featherston Street for seven blocks to the intersection with Panama Street. Turn left onto Panama and cross **Customhouse Quay** to the Queen's Wharf waterfront and TSB Bank Arena (tel: 04 801 4231; www.wellington conventioncentre.com), where a trip to a museum is next on the agenda.

Museum of Wellington City and Sea
Located next to the Customhouse Quay entrance to Queen's Wharf, the **Museum of Wellington City and Sea** ❽ (Queens Wharf; tel: 04 472 8904; www.museumofwellington.co.nz; daily 10am–5pm; free) has a captivating collection of maritime memorabilia, covering the city's seafaring history

Vibrant Food Scene
Wellingtonians love their coffee and have a fabulous café culture. Those with an appetite for culinary adventure can discover more about Wellington's vibrant food scene on a Zest Food Tour (tel: 04 801 9198). Guides introduce you to their favourite Wellington gourmet food stores, coffee roasters, cafés and restaurants, and provide the chance to savour many often-missed local delicacies.

Food and Drink

① NIKAU GALLERY CAFÉ
City Gallery Building, Civic Square; tel: 04 801 4168; $
Contemporary café with floor-to-ceiling windows and a sheltered, sun-drenched courtyard. Coffee, wine, snacks and light lunches are served here.

② CAFFE ASTORIA
159 Lambton Quay; tel: 04 473 8500; $$
Reminiscent of a Viennese coffee house, this café is a favourite haunt of the corporate crowd. Come here for snacks, light lunches and dinner and, of course, the coffee.

③ SKYLINE CAFÉ
1 Upland Road; tel: 04 475 8727; $$
Accessed by cable car, this is a top choice for lunch for its fine views over the city. Fresh, light lunches and good cocktails.

④ BACKBENCHER
34 Molesworth Street; tel: 04 472 3065; wwww.backbencher. co.nz; 11am–late; $$
Everything, including the menu, at this pub has a political theme, and the walls are decorated with cartoons and caricatures of local political figures.

Above from left: the Westpac St James Theatre; at a Martinborough vineyard.

Katherine Mansfield
The writer, one of Wellington's most famous daughters, was born Kathleen Mansfield Beauchamp in 1888 to a middle-class colonial family. She was partly schooled in England and left New Zealand permanently for there at the age of 18 with the support of £100 a year from her father. In England, she moved in bohemian literary circles that included such writers as Virginia Woolf and D.H. Lawrence. She was married twice, firstly to George Brown, then to literary critic John Murray. Under the pen-name Katherine Mansfield, she wrote collections of short stories, notably *Prelude, Bliss* and *The Garden Party*. She died of tuberculosis in 1923. To find out more about her, visit the restored two-storey family home in which she was born, the Katherine Mansfield Birthplace (25 Tinakori Road; tel: 04 473 7268; www.katherine mansfield.com; Tue–Sun 10am–4pm; charge), in the Wellington district of Thorndon.

from early Maori interaction to the 1900s. Highlights include a 12-minute show retelling Maori creation stories. After touring the museum, pop into **Shed 5**, see ⑤, for refreshments.

ORIENTAL PARADE

If you still have time on your side, and the weather is good, walk back to Museum of New Zealand, then carry on around the waterfront following Cable Street to **Oriental Parade ❾**. Here a stroll around the boardwalk gives great views over the city; note Wellington's prime residential real estate clinging to the slopes of Mount Victoria. Call at the **Parade Café**, see ⑥, for refreshments.

COURTENAY PLACE

Return via Courtenay Place, Wellington's main entertainment precinct. At the intersection with Kent Terrace is the grand old **Embassy Theatre**, venue of the world première of the final cinematic installment of *The Lord of the Rings* trilogy. Further up Courtenay Place on the left is the **Westpac St James Theatre** (77–87 Courtenay Place; tel: 04 802 6917; www.stjames.co. nz), which hosts musical acts and is home to the **Jimmy Café and Bar**, see ⑦. Dinner options nearby include **King Wah**, see ⑧, on Courtenay Place and the **Satay Indian Bistro**, see ⑨, around the corner on Allen Street.

Food and Drink

⑤ SHED 5
Queens Wharf; tel: 04 499 9069; $$
Upmarket seafood restaurant, café and bar set inside a restored late-19th-century woolshed, with waterfront outdoor seating. Thai fishcakes are the house speciality.

⑥ PARADE CAFÉ
148 Oriental Parade; tel: 04 939 3935; $
Popular café and restaurant in a great location on this attractive seafront promenade. An open fire in winter and a sunny courtyard in summer. Great food at low prices with an eclectic ambience.

⑦ JIMMY CAFÉ AND BAR
Westpac St James Theatre, Courtenay Place; tel: 04 802 6930; $
Located just inside the entrance to the theatre, this is the perfect place to conclude the day's sightseeing and plan your evening's entertainment over a coffee.

⑧ KING WAH
27 Courtenay Place; tel: 04 801 5657; $
Admire the rich red decor, fish tanks and tables with lazy susans. Serves some of the best Chinese food in the city. Yum char is on offer at lunch on Sundays.

⑨ SATAY INDIA BISTRO
18 Allen Street; tel: 04 385 7709; $
Locals throng here for cheap, tasty Malaysian and Indian food.

THE WAIRARAPA

This tour takes you out of Wellington, over the Rimutaka Ranges and into the Wairarapa region. Highlights include Martinborough's vineyards, Greytown's colonial architecture and the imposing, rugged coastline.

The scenery of the southern Wairarapa region is ruggedly dramatic: rolling tablelands end abruptly to form high, textured cliffs, the Rimutaka Ranges cast shadows over Lake Wairarapa, and, to the north, the Tararua Ranges tower over fertile plains. At the centre of this is Martinborough, a town that is internationally recognised for its pinot noir.

Wellington to Featherston

Start in **Wellington ❶**, at the railway station on Bunny Street. Turn left on to Waterloo Quay, driving past the Westpac Trust Stadium and following signs to the Wellington/Hutt motorway. This takes you along the western edge of Wellington Harbour. There are several sets of traffic lights to slow your progress through Lower Hutt, Stokes Valley and Upper Hutt. From here SH2 begins its windy climb over the Rimutaka Ranges. Stop at the top for views of the range's bush-clad hills and, beyond, to the plains of the Wairarapa.

FEATHERSTON

A 16-km (10-mile) drive brings you to the town of **Featherston ❷**, where you can pick up regional information from the **Featherston Visitor Centre** (tel: 06 308 8051; www.wairarapanz.com; daily 10am–3pm), housed in the Old Court-

DISTANCE 202km (125 miles) return or 346km (214 miles) including the South Coast
TIME At least one day
START/END Wellington
POINTS TO NOTE
You will need a car for this tour; for details of car-hire firms, *see p.111.* Martinborough is an 81-km (50-mile) drive from Wellington, but the tour takes longer than expected because the road over the Rimutaka Ranges is so winding. To avoid rush-hour congestion, leave very early (around 6.30am) or head off after 9am.

Above: signs of historic Greytown.

house building on Fitzherbert Street. On the corner of Fitzherbert and Lyon streets is Featherston's main attraction, the **Fell Engine Museum** (tel: 06 308 9379; daily 10am–4pm; charge), home to the only Fell locomotive in the world.

POW Memorial

Now continue north on SH2. Just 1km (²⁄₃ mile) past Featherston you will pass a **POW Memorial**; it is on the site of a former World War I army training barracks, which was also used to hold Japanese soldiers captured in the Solomon Islands during World War II. In an attempted breakout

Drink Driving
The legal limit for drinking when driving is a blood alcohol content of 0.08 percent for those over 20 years old and 0.03 percent for those under 20 years old. There is a low tolerance of over-stepping these limits, so the advice is not to drink and drive at all.

Divine Chocolate
Next door to the Cobblestones Museum is the divine chocolatier, Schoc Chocolates (177 Main Street, Greytown; tel: 06 304 8960; www.chocolatetherapy.com; Mon–Fri 10am–5pm, Sat–Sun 10.30am–5pm), where organic and preservative-free chocolates and truffles are made on site. Deliciously bitter dark chocolate is a speciality, and their signature lime-chilli range is all the rage in these parts.

from the camp in 1943, some 48 prisoners lost their lives.

GREYTOWN

A further 15-km (9-mile) drive brings you to **Greytown 3**, New Zealand's first planned inland town. Despite its name, it is anything but colourless; its main street is lined with fine examples of early New Zealand wooden Victorian architecture. Spend time browsing its boutiques, where you can buy anything from an 18th-century chair and Italian earrings to designer clothes and locally produced art. On the main street, **Salute**, see ⑪①, is a good for an early lunch; alternatively, save yourself for **The Old Winery Café** *(see opposite)*.

The **Cobblestones Museum** (169 Main Street; tel: 06 304 9687; Mon–Fri 9am–5pm, Sat–Sun 10am–4pm; charge) provides a fascinating insight into the region's past. Here you can see Greytown's first Methodist church, erected in 1868; a 100-year-old threshing machine; the intact Mangapakeha school (a single-teacher school, opened in 1902), and the Wairarapa's first public hospital, which dates to 1875. The atmospheric old coaching stables and cobbled grounds (1857) make it easy to imagine the clip-clop of hoofs as old stage coaches pulled up here with cargoes of new pioneers.

While you're exploring Greytown look out for the enormous eucalyptus tree outside St Luke's Church, on Main Street. The story goes that Samuel Oates brought the first wheeled vehicle (a wheelbarrow) over the Rimutakas 150 years ago, bearing a cargo of seedlings. Three seedlings 'disappeared' in Greytown, and the results are easy to spot.

MARTINBOROUGH

Any visit to the Wairarapa is incomplete without paying a visit to the township of **Martinborough 4**, the hub of the wine industry, a short drive from Greytown. Drive south down Greytown's Main Street and veer left off SH2. You will pass several vineyards on the way into Martinborough, as well as the local **Information Centre** (18 Kitchener Street; tel: 06 306 5010; www.wairarapanz.com; daily 10am–4pm).

Wine Tours

With so many vineyards to choose from, the **Martinborough Wine Centre** (6 Kitchener Street; tel: 06 306 9040; www.martinboroughwinecentre.co.nz;

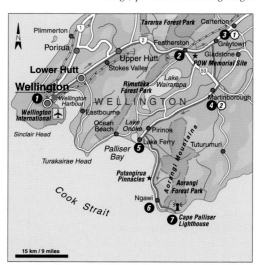

daily 10am–5pm; free), in the centre of the town, is a good place to start. Here, you can sample a variety of wine from local vineyards and arm yourself with a copy of the Wairarapa and Martinborough wine trail map, ready to explore.

There are around 24 wineries within walking distance of the centre, including **Palliser Estate** (Martins Road; tel: 06 306 9019; www.palliser.co.nz; Mon–Fri 10.30am–4pm, Sat–Sun 10.30am–5pm) and **Te Kairanga** (Martins Road; tel: 06 306 9122; www.tkwine.co.nz; daily 10am–5pm), both on Martins Road, running southeast of the centre.

Hold out for lunch, though at **The Old Winery Café**, see ⑪②, on Ponatahi Road, which leads northeast out of Martinborough.

TOWARDS LAKE FERRY

The remainder of the day can be spent sampling wine, perusing local arts and crafts or discovering the scenic south coast. To do this, leave Martinborough on the Lake Ferry Road and head south to **Lake Ferry** ❺, a small settlement with contrasting views over the pounding waves of **Palliser Bay** and tranquil waters of **Lake Onoke**.

Putangirua Pinnacles and Ngawi
Continue on, with the sea on your right, to the **Putangirua Pinnacles** (free), huge, organ pipe-like columns that were formed over the past 120,000 years by heavy rain washing away silt and sand to expose the underlying bedrock.

Further on, in **Ngawi** ❻, a picturesque fishing village at the base of the towering **Aorangi Range**, rows of brightly painted bulldozers park on the beach. The town does not have a natural harbour, so the bulldozers are used to launch fishing boats from the beach. Keep your eyes open along this coastline for seals *(see right)*.

Cape Palliser Lighthouse
Pick up the same road you were driving on and continue south. High on the edge of a weather-beaten cliff, is the **Cape Palliser Lighthouse** ❼, constructed in 1896 from materials brought here by boat and marking the southernmost point of the North Island. Hike the 258 steep steps to the top, from where you can gain magnificent views across the Cook Strait to the snow-capped mountains of Kaikoura.

End of the Tour
On the return journey, if it's getting late, consider spending a night at the elegant colonial-style **Peppers Martinborough Hotel** *(see p.115)*; alternatively take SH53 to Featherston, where you can pick up SH2 back to Wellington.

Above from far left: colonial architecture; the apple industry is big in this part of the country; keep an eye out for seals in Ngawi, but be sure to maintain the recommended distance of 10m (33ft); Cape Palliser Lighthouse.

Winemakers
The Wairarapa region produces about 3,000 cases of wine per year and is particularly successful with the pinot noir grape. On the wave of Martinborough's wine boom, a flurry of boutique vineyards have opened in the north in Gladstone, East Taratahi, Masterton and Te Puna.

Food and Drink

① SALUTE
83 Main Street, Greytown; tel: 06 304 9828; $$
This unpretentious place offers robust Middle Eastern flavours and fine wines that can be enjoyed next to a log fire on chilly Wairarapa winter days or under shady oaks outside in summer.

② THE OLD WINERY CAFÉ
Corner of Ponatahi and Huangarua roads; tel: 06 306 8333; www.theoldwinerycafe.co.nz; $–$$
Located next to the Margrain Vineyard, the Old Winery Café matches fresh local cuisine with a superb range of local wines.

FERRY TO THE SOUTH ISLAND

Cruise across the scenic Cook Strait, keeping your eyes peeled for dolphins, seals and seabirds. Visit the vineyards of Blenheim in the heart of the Marlborough wine country, and either stay overnight there or return to Wellington.

Below: on a whale-watching tour.

Using **Wellington ❶** as a base, you can make a day trip to Picton in the South Island, visit the wineries of Blenheim and return to Wellington later in the day. The tour can either be done as an organised trip or an independent drive; the information below explains what to expect from both options.

ORGANISED TOURS

The Interislander (tel: 0800 802 802; www.interislandline.co.nz; call centre Mon–Fri 8am–8pm, Sat–Sun 8am–6pm) offers this trip – which is somewhat confusingly called the 'Half Day Marlborough Wine Trail', although it is actually a full-day tour – aboard the MV *Kaitaki*. Check-in is at 8am for an 8.25am departure, with a scheduled arrival time in Picton of around 11.35am.

Picton and Blenheim
The early arrival leaves plenty of time to explore the waterfront area in **Picton ❷**, where attractions include the **EcoWorld** aquarium (Dunbar Wharf; tel: 03 573 6030; www.ecoworldnz.co.nz; charge), the **Edwin Fox Maritime Museum** (Dunbar Wharf;

tel: 03 573 6868; www.edwinfoxsociety. com; daily from 9am; charge), documenting the history of the world's ninth-oldest ship, plus shops and cafés, such as **Le Café**, see ⓧⓘ, on London Quay, close to the Town Wharf.

At 1.30pm a guided tour departs from the **Sounds Connection Office** (10 London Quay) bound for the vineyards of **Blenheim** ❸, where there's a chance to taste a selection of wines from four of the region's top vineyards, including Montana, the largest winery in Marlborough. If you have a particular interest in a winery, it's worth letting your guide know, as they will endeavour to incorporate it into the allocated time-frame.

The wine-tasting tour concludes at 5.30pm at the Picton terminal, ready for the return journey to Wellington on the MV *Aratere* at 6pm (arrives Wellington 9pm; meals are available on board). Alternatively, you can elect to remain in Picton until 9.35pm, for a ferry departure on the MV *Arahura* at 10pm (arrives Wellington 1am). The latter option provides the opportunity to enjoy a leisurely evening meal in Picton.

SELF-DRIVES

If you've rented a car, take it on the ferry with you, or hire a car in Picton. Some rental companies allow you to leave your North Island vehicle in Wellington and pick up a new car in Picton. If you are taking your vehicle across, The Interislander *(see opposite)* is one of two major companies travelling the Cook Strait between Wellington and Picton; the other is Bluebridge (tel: 0800 844 844; www.blue bridge.co.nz).

Picton and Blenheim

When you arrive in **Picton**, visit the **i-SITE Visitor Centre** (Lagoon

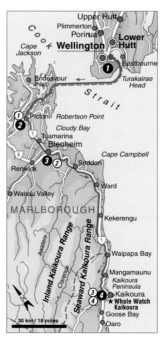

Above from far left: spectacular Kaikoura; Marlborough wine country, at the northern tip of the South Island.

Picton Township
The main attraction of Picton township is soaking up the atmosphere of its buzzing foreshore. Here, kids can sail model yachts in a small pool for 20c a pop, and there's a playground, a merry-go-round, an 18-hole mini golf course, and the Seahorse World Aquarium (Dunbar Wharf, Picton Foreshore; tel: 03 573 6030; www. seahorseworld.co.nz; daily, 9am–6pm; charge), with shark and crayfish feeding sessions, touch pools and all-day tickets, so you can come and go as you please.

Food and Drink ⓧ
① LE CAFÉ
London Quay, Picton; tel: 03 573 5588; $
If you're hanging out for vegetables order the 'BFS' (Big Fat Salad), which comes served with brie, olives and fresh breads – with a side order of local mussels. Everything is home-made here, even the lollies.

Above from left: whales can be identified by their tails; punting in Christchurch, a city that delights in tradition.

Whale-Spotting

At Kaikoura the chances of spotting a whale are good, thanks to high-tech tracking devices. The sonar 'clicks' from the submerged animals are tracked by a sensitive hydrophone, so the boat can be positioned roughly where the whale will resurface for around 10 minutes, taking breaths before it submerges again. The best part is when the leviathan throws up its flukes and disappears.

Road; tel: 03 520 3113; www.picton.co.nz) on the town's foreshore for maps and information, then drive south on SH1 to **Blenheim**, where you can choose to visit any number of wineries producing some of the country's finest sauvignon blanc. Consider eating at **Montana Brancott**, see ⑪②.

Kaikoura

Now continue on SH1 to **Kaikoura ❹** on the South Island's East Coast. 'Kaikoura' means 'crayfish food', a name given because of the region's bountiful sea life: sample some at the local restaurants, see ⑪③. If seafood is not to your taste, the excellent **Hislops Café**, see ⑪④, is a good alternative.

Whale-Watching

A highlight of this part of New Zealand is a tour with **Whale Watch Kaikoura**

(Waterfront; tel: 0800 655 121; www.whalewatch.co.nz; tours daily 7.15am, 10am, 12.45pm and Nov–Mar 3.30pm; charge). Trips take 2½ hours, and head offshore to view some of the world's biggest mammals in their natural environment. **Whale Watch** is the country's only marine-based whale-watching company, offering close encounters with whales (usually sperm whales in this part of the country) at all times of the year – if you don't see a whale, 80 percent of your tour price will be refunded.

Dolphin Tours

You can also frolic with dolphins on a trip out to sea with **Dolphin Encounters** (96 The Esplanade, Kaikoura; tel: 0800 733 365; www.dolphin.co.nz; summer 5.30am, 8.30am, 12.30pm, winter 8.30am, 12.30pm; charge). Allow 3 to 3½ hours for the tour.

Food and Drink 🍴

② MONTANA BRANCOTT
SH1, Riverlands, Blenheim; tel: 03 577 5775; $$
Brancott's serves a variety of fresh dishes, each expertly teamed with a matching Marlborough wine. There's indoor and outdoor dining, and families are well catered for with an adjoining 'wine-themed' playground, complete with corkscrew slide.

③ WHITE MORPH
92 Esplanade, Kaikoura; tel: 03 319 5014; $$–$$$
Look no further for the freshest fish, crayfish and Pacific Rim cuisine perfectly matched to a selection of local wines.

④ HISLOPS CAFÉ
33 Beach Road, Kaikoura; tel: 03 319 6971; $
Hislops specialises in wholefoods and organics and has an extensive menu with substantial meat, vegetarian, vegan and gluten-free options. It's also a great place to pick up genuine stoneground wholemeal bread (baked daily) for the picnic basket, and enjoy coffee teamed with still-warm muffins.

Whaling

Historic Fyffe House in Kaikoura is the town's oldest surviving building and is located close to where Robert Fyffe established the first shore-based whaling station in 1842. Other stations were subsequently built, and at one stage the industry employed over 100 men. In the 1850s, whale numbers declined, but the industry continued in New Zealand until 1964. In 1978, the Marine Mammal Protection Act was passed, providing total protection to all of New Zealand's whales, dolphins and seals.

CHRISTCHURCH

This is a walking tour of elegant Christchurch, dubbed as New Zealand's Garden City, for its proliferation of cultivated gardens. The city prides itself on its strong English roots and, true to British tradition, you may even spot the odd eccentric here.

Christchurch (pop. about 344,000) has been described so often as 'the most English city outside England' that the term has become a cliché. Yet the comparison is inescapable. Conceived as an outpost of Anglicanism and laid out on the lines of an English university town around a cathedral, Christchurch was planned as a haven of quiet gardens and calm, orderly ways. The first settlers (called the Canterbury Pilgrims after the province in which Christchurch is situated) disembarked in Lyttelton Harbour in 1850. They had been specially selected by their hometown ministers, who were urged to ensure that all the pilgrims be sober, industrious, honest – and under 40. Inland, on a plain in the Canterbury district, they found their town ready-planned and endowed with nostalgic street names.

Christchurch rapidly became the centre of a prosperous farming region. By the mid-1860s a million sheep grazed in Canterbury pastures. Today, Canterbury lamb is extensively exported, and the area rates as the country's chief grain producer.

CATHEDRAL SQUARE

At the heart of the grid system on which central Christchurch is built is

DISTANCE 3km (2 miles)
TIME A full day
START Cathedral Square
END Cashel Mall
POINTS TO NOTE
Within easy drives of Christchurch are the vineyards of Waipara, scenic Arthur's Pass, skiing at Mount Hutt, and the Banks Peninsula, with its French-inspired seaside resort of Akaroa, so consider using the city as a base for tours 12–14.

Cathedral Square ❶, where this day-long walking tour commences. The pedestrian-only square is officially regarded, in the style of London's Hyde Park, as a public-speaking area.

Garden City
The 'Garden City' label was made official in 1997, when Christchurch was named Garden City of the World. It's especially beautiful in late summer.

Historic Tram Tour

Christchurch has an historic tram (tel: 03 366 7830; www.tram.co.nz; daily, Apr–Oct 9am–6pm, Nov–Mar 9am–9pm) that does a circuit from Cathedral Square to the Arts Centre, Canterbury Museum, Christ's College, Victoria Square, New Regent Street and back to Cathedral Square. It is worth doing a full circuit to get your bearings before venturing out on foot, or, if the weather is bad, simply use the tram to explore the city, hopping on and off at all its stops.

First Inhabitants

Maori oral history suggests that people first inhabited the Canterbury area about 1,000 years ago and hunted the now extinct moa, a flightless, ostrich-like bird. The first European landed in Canterbury in 1815, 45 years after Captain James Cook sighted what he named 'Banks Island', which was later discovered to be a peninsula.

Star performer is The Wizard (www.wizard.gen.nz), Australian-born Ian Brackenbury Channell, who has long been appearing at the Square (usually lunchtime in summer) to harangue bemused crowds. Dressed in black robes, he delivers an impassioned line on topics ranging from Queen and country (for) through feminism (against) to his view of the causes of global warming.

Other highlights in the square include the year-round market (Wed–Sat 10am–4pm). There's also the **Christchurch i-SITE Visitor Centre** (tel: 03 379 9629; www.christchurchnz.net; Mon–Fri 8.30am–5pm, Sat–Sun 8.30am–4.30pm).

Christchurch Cathedral

Situated on the east side of the square is the imposing neo-Gothic **Christ-church Cathedral** (tel: 03 379 0046; www.christchurchcathedral.co.nz; Mon–Sat 8.30am–5pm, Sun 7.30am–5pm; tours Mon–Fri 11am and 2pm, Sat 11am, Sun 11.30am; free).

Dating to the mid-19th century, it is one of the southern hemisphere's finest neo-Gothic churches. Building began in 1864 but halted soon after due to a lack of funds. Some argued that the Church had better things to spend its money on – a recurring theme in New Zealand ecclesiastical building history – and construction only began again when the bishop of the time promised to contribute some of his own salary. The cathedral was finally completed in 1904, and a visitor centre was added 90 years later. For a small charge, climb the 134 steps up the 63-m (208-ft) tower past the belfry for breathtaking city views.

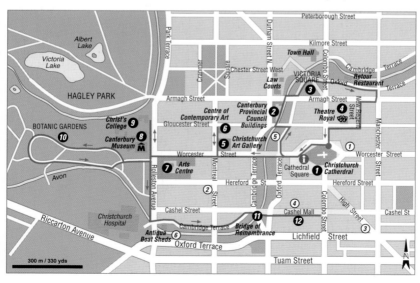

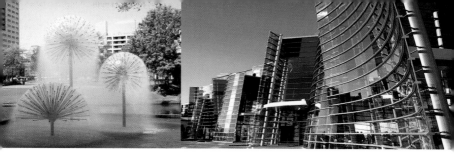

VICTORIA SQUARE

Now head north along Oxford Terrace and follow the river all the way to Gloucester Street. Turn left and cross the Gloucester Street Bridge. Here you will see a pathway that leads along the Avon River's west bank beside the **Canterbury Provincial Council Buildings** ❷ (corner of Durham and Armagh streets; tel: 03 941 7680; guided tours Mon–Sat 10.30am–3pm). These are the only remaining provincial government buildings in New Zealand.

A 100-m (109-yd) walk brings you out on to Armagh Street, opposite the Law Courts, and if you cross back over the river you will arrive at **Victoria Square** ❸, a restful expanse of green, anchored by the Town Hall. Opened in 1972, after the city had dithered for 122 years over a civic centre, this building remains the pride of modern Christchurch. Designed by local architects Warren and Mahoney, it is restrained and elegant, with an auditorium, concert hall, conference rooms and a restaurant.

Take a stroll around the square, noting the statues of Queen Victoria and Captain Cook in front of Hamish Hay Bridge. Built in 1863, this was the first cast-iron-and-stone bridge of its type in New Zealand.

ALONG THE AVON RIVER

Leave Victoria Square by crossing over Colombo Street and following Oxford Terrace, as it resumes its way winding along the banks of the river. On your left note on Cambridge Terrace the beautifully restored **Retour Restaurant** *(see p.122)*, converted from a band rotunda. Punts can be hired from just near here.

Now turn right into Manchester Street, right again into Armagh Street, and then left into New Regent Street (closed to vehicles except trams). This pretty street has attractive Edwardian façades painted in delicate pastel blues and yellows, and cafés and shops lining its pavements.

Turn right into Gloucester Street past the **Theatre Royal** ❹ and then first left into Colombo Street and you are back at Cathedral Square, where **Octagon**, see ⑪①, is a grand venue for lunch.

CHRISTCHURCH ART GALLERY

From Cathedral Square, walk west along Worcester Boulevard (note the statue of the city's founder John Robert Godley at the exit to the square at this point). Cross the river and follow the tram route for one block. At the corner of Montreal Street is **Christchurch Art Gallery** ❺ (tel: 03 941 7300; www.christchurchartgallery.

Above from far left: the river in autumn; Cathedral Square, the heart of Christchurch; fountains in the Avon River; Christchurch Art Gallery.

Above: cherry blossom in Hagley Park; punting along the river; view of Christchurch from the waterfront.

Food and Drink 🍴

① OCTAGON
Worcester Street; tel: 03 366 6171; $$$
Housed in a striking Gothic building built for a congregation of 37 members in 1874, this upmarket place does exquisite seafood and frequently presents live music.

Mona Vale

The late-Victorian homestead of Mona Vale (63 Fendalton Road, Riccarton; tel: 03 348 9660; www. monavale.co.nz; charge) is a delightful place to combine a walk around its gardens with some lunch or a tea break. The homestead was once owned by the Deans, one of Christchurch's first settler families.

org.nz; Thur–Tue 10am–5pm, Wed 10am–9pm; charge). The largest public art gallery in the South Island, it houses a permanent collection of paintings, sculpture and ceramics, and holds regular special exhibits.

CENTRE OF CONTEMPORARY ART

Contemporary art fans should take the first right after the gallery, Montreal Street, and head one block north to Gloucester Street. Just on the right,

at no.66, is the **Centre of Contemporary Art ❻** (tel: 03 366 7261; www. coca.org.nz; donation appreciated), the city's main showcase for contemporary art, established in 1880. Its five galleries, spread over three floors, host more than 60 exhibitions per year and provide a fascinating insight into both New Zealand and Canterburian modern art. The centre also hosts an extensive 'Open Gallery', where hundreds of artworks by New Zealand artists are displayed for purchase.

ARTS CENTRE

Allow 30 minutes to an hour here, then continue west along Worcester Street for one block until you reach the **Arts Centre ❼** (daily 9.30am–5pm, 10am–3.30pm; free), housed in neo-Gothic stone buildings and a mass of dreaming spires, turrets and cloisters – formerly part of Canterbury University.

The Arts Centre is a focal point for local artisans and craftspeople, and the whole area comes alive at the busy Sunday market (10am–4pm). Other attractions here include the **Court Theatre**, the restored den of the Nobel Prize-winning scientist Ernest Rutherford *(see right)*, and the arthouse **Academy Cinema** (tel: 03 366 0167; www.artfilms.co.nz/academy).

There are also a wide variety of craft studios and boutique food outlets within the complex, so take your time to soak up the artistic atmosphere. If the cafés aren't quite to your taste, you could also try the nearby **Dux de Lux**, see ⑪②.

Food and Drink 🍴

② THE DUX DE LUX
Corner of Hereford and Montreal streets; tel: 03 366 6919; $
Popular restaurant/bar, with a huge open courtyard, award-winning house-brewed beer and live music, including jazz on Tuesday. The eclectic menu includes local seafood, pizzas and salads.

③ HONEYPOT CAFE
114 Lichfield Street; tel: 03 366 5853; $
Casual eatery serving full meals as well as a selection of delicious sandwiches and pizzas with innovative toppings such as tandoori chicken and Cajun and sour-cream sauce. Great desserts and coffee too, all at affordable prices.

④ VIA DEL CORSO
114 Cashel Mall; tel: 03 377 5001; $–$$
Well-priced, mouthwatering Italian food: pane, antipasti, soups, pastas and baked dishes. Live music in the evenings.

⑤ CAFFE ROMA
176 Oxford Terrace; tel: 03 379 3879; $
Housed inside what was once a Gentleman's Club, this European-style café serves good coffee, brunch and lunch within its old-world setting of wood panelling and high ceilings. It's a good place to curl up beside the stone fireplace with plenty of reading material.

⑥ PEGASUS ARMS
14 Oxford Terrace; tel 03 366 0600; $
The Pegasus Arms is housed in an historic building that dates to 1851. The menu is a list of enticing pub classics.

CANTERBURY MUSEUM

Next on the itinerary is the **Canterbury Museum** ❽ (tel: 03 366 5000; www. canterburymuseum.com; daily Oct–Mar 9am–5.30pm, Apr–Sept 9am–5pm; guided tours Tue and Thur 3.30–4.30pm; charge), at the end of Worcester Street, on Rolleston Avenue. Besides displays exploring Canterbury's pre-European and pioneer history and showcasing a fine collection of European decorative art and costume, the museum also devotes space to the discovery and exploration of Antarctica, and to **Discovery**, the museum's natural history centre for children.

BOTANIC GARDENS

North of the museum is **Christ's College** ❾, a private boys' school with wide landscaped grounds. To the south and west, enclosed within a loop of the Avon River as it winds through the 161-ha (500-acre) **Hagley Park** (originally created to separate city and farmland) are the 30-ha (74-acre) **Botanic Gardens** ❿ (daily 7am–sunset; tel: 03 941 6840; www.ccc.govt. nz/parks; free), one of the finest in the world, established in 1863. Highlights include the English herbaceous borders, native sections, and glasshouses of subtropical and desert specimens.

TOWARDS CASHEL MALL

Leave the gardens and head right along Rolleston Avenue, rejoining the Avon River by the Christchurch Hospital. If you have the energy, try a popular local family pastime, paddling on the river; boats for this are available for hire from the **Antigua Boat Sheds** (2 Cambridge Terrace; tel: 03 366 5885; www. boat-sheds.co.nz; daily, summer 9.30am–5.30pm, winter 9.30am–4pm; charge).

Cashel Mall

After 200m (218yds) up Rolleston Avenue, you will hit Montreal Street. Turn right and walk two blocks to Cashel Street, then turn right. Ahead is the archway of the **Bridge of Remembrance** ⓫, a World War I memorial. Cross the bridge into the pedestrian-only **Cashel Mall** ⓬, lined with shops, cafés and bars. End your tour here, or on nearby Oxford Terrace or Lichfield Street, which are also good for drinks and dinner; see ⑪③–⑥.

Ernest Rutherford

Born in Nelson, in the north of the South Island, in 1871, Ernest Rutherford became the first person to split the atom and was awarded the Nobel Prize for Chemistry in 1908. He died in Cambridge, Britain, in 1937. He looks pensively from the $100 note that bills him as Lord Rutherford of Nelson.

Port Hillls

To finish your day in Christchurch on a high note, ride up the Port Hills with Christchurch Gondola (10 Bridle Path Road; tel: 03 384 0700; www.gondola.co.nz; daily 10am–9pm; charge). To get there, take the Gondola Bus, a regular, free shuttle bus service from the city centre. Disembark at the Gondola Terminal for the 500-m (1,640-ft) ride to the rim of the now-extinct Lyttelton Volcano. On clear days, there are spectacular views from the gallery at the summit; there's also a restaurant and souvenir shops. The ride back is equally compelling, but hardier types might consider hiring a mountain bike for an alternative route down.

AKAROA

Spend a day discovering the Banks Peninsula and the attractive French-inspired settlement of Akaroa on this driving tour. Take a harbour cruise and enjoy a leisurely lunch overlooking the harbour before returning to Christchurch in the late afternoon.

DISTANCE 168km (104 miles) return

TIME A full day

START/END Christchurch

POINTS TO NOTE

You will need a car for this tour; for details of car-hire firms, *see p.111*.

If you leave early, there will be time to return to Christchurch via Summit Road, Diamond Harbour and Lyttelton, a scenic route that completes a loop around the Banks Peninsula.

Below: swing tyre at Lake Ellesmere.

Located around 80km (50 miles) from Christchurch, the little settlement of Akaroa began its European life in 1838, when a French whaler, Captain Jean-François Langlois, landed on its shores and bought – or so he thought – Banks Peninsula from the Maori. Sixty-three settlers set out from France on the *Comte de Paris* to create a South Seas outpost. But they arrived in 1840 to find the Union Jack flying. Pipped at the colonial post, the French settlers nevertheless stayed. They planted poplars from Normandy, named streets after places in their home country and grew grapes, but by 1843, they were outnumbered by the English.

The French dream lingers on though, and has been brushed up for visitors. Little streets, with names such as Rue Lavaud and Rue Jolie, wind up the hill from the harbourfront. A charming colonial style predominates, and has been protected by town-planning rules.

CHRISTCHURCH TO BARRY'S BAY

From Cathedral Square in **Christchurch ❶**, head south along Colombo Street to Moorhouse Avenue. Turn right and travel to the end of the road, where it connects with a corner of

ma maison deli

Hagley Park. Follow the sign left into Lincoln Road (to **Lincoln ❷**), over the railway line and out on to what becomes SH75, travelling through the farmlands of Halswell, Taitapu and Motukarara.

Birdlings Flat

Here the road travels alongside Lake Ellesmere (Waihora), a wide, shallow coastal lagoon that attracts game birds and waterfowl, before taking a sharp turn left at the turn-off for **Birdlings Flat**. Take a short sidetrip here out to the beach, where the ocean transforms stones such as rose quartz into polished gems, and deposits them on the stony beach, ready to fossick. To see examples of the precious gems found on these shores, visit the local **Gemstone and Fossil Museum** (SH75; www.birdlingsmuseum.741.com; Sun–Fri 10am–4.30pm; free).

Little River and Hilltop

Back on SH75 continue past picturesque Lake Forsyth to the small settlement of **Little River ❸**, once a notable stop on the old railway line through this part of the Banks Peninsula.

The road climbs steeply out of Cooptown up to **Hilltop ❹** and the Hilltop

Tavern, whose car park offers grand views over the Onawe Peninsula, which extends into the Akaroa Harbour. This was the site of a Maori *pa* (fortified village), built in 1831 by the Ngai Tahu people to stave off a northern tribe.

Barry's Bay

Continue into **Barry's Bay ❺**, where you can make a stop at Barry's Bay Cheese (Main Road, Barry's Bay; tel: 03 304 5809) to sample their traditionally hand-crafted products and watch the cheese-making process through glass windows, before travelling on through Duvauchelle and Takamatua to **Akaroa ❻**. (Note that a good place to stop is the **French Farm Winery**, see ⑪①, west of the turn-off to the cheese factory.)

AKAROA

Park as soon as you enter the town – there's plenty of free parking available – and walk along Rue Lavaud.

Above from far left: the Akaroa Peninsula; French cuisine in Akaroa.

Food and Drink ⑪

① FRENCH FARM WINERY

French Farm Valley Road, Akaroa; tel: 03 304 5784; $$
Enjoy a casual alfresco lunch dining on wood-fired pizza, or indulge in French provincial cuisine teamed with local wine in the cosy dining room.

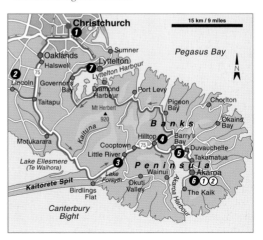

Akaroa Museum

Make your first stop the **Akaroa Museum** (tel: 03 304 7614; daily 10.30am–4.30pm; charge), situated at the corner of Rue Lavaud and Rue Balguerie. Here, highlights include Maori *taonga* (treasures), as well as relics from Akaroa's whaling past. A 20-minute audio-visual relates the complete history of the town.

Langlois-Eteveneaux Cottage

The museum also incorporates several of the town's important historical buildings, including the Customs House at Daly's Wharf and the **Langlois-Eteve-neaux Cottage** (corner of Rue Lavaud and Rue Balguerie; tel: 03 304 1013; www.nzmuseums.co.nz; daily: winter 10.30am–4pm, summer 10.30am–4.30pm; charge). The cottage, which was pre-fabricated in France, is one of the oldest in Canterbury.

Other Sights

After visiting the museum, take a walk along Rue Balguerie to **St Patrick's Church**, built in 1863, then continue on up Rue Balgueri to Settlers Hill, where a track will lead you to L'Aube Hill Reserve and the **Old French Cemetery**, the first consecrated burial ground in Canterbury.

Next, walk back to Rue Lavaud and enjoy a stroll through its gardens, past the centrepiece **War Memorial** to the sweeping beachside promenade. On a sunny day it's lovely to leave the car

Right: Akaroa lighthouse.

and walk around the bay to the English part of town, taking in the views across the inlet.

Alternatively you can drive the same route and park near the **Akaroa wharf**, a popular place for fishing.

Akaroa Harbour

It is now time to head for **Akaroa Harbour**. Sign up at the wharf for a harbour cruise aboard **Black Cat Cruises** (tel: 03 304 7641; www. blackcat.co.nz; daily Nov–Apr 11am and 1pm, May–Oct 11am; charge), which explores Akaroa's deep, sea-filled crater.

On the two-hour trip to the headlands you will visit a salmon farm and spot dolphins, fur seals and a variety of sea birds, such as the little blue penguin. The company also provides the only opportunity in New Zealand to swim with the Hector's (or NZ) dolphin (Nov–Apr 6am, 8.30am, 11.30am, 1.30pm, 3.30pm, May–Oct 11.30am). This is one of the world's smallest and rarest dolphin species, with a total population of around 6,000–7,000 animals.

After the cruise, if the timing's right, take time out to sample the fresh catch of the day and the excellent local wines at cafés, including **Bully Hayes**, see ①②, by the waterfront.

BACK TO CHRISTCHURCH

To return to Christchurch, there are two options: either retrace your route through Little River, Motukarara, Taitapu and Halswell or, for a two-hour scenic drive of Banks Peninsula, go back to Christchurch via the attractive port of **Lyttelton** ❼.

For the route through Lyttelton, take the signposted Summit Road, which offers gorgeous scenic views, and follow the signs to Lyttelton travelling through Pigeon Bay, Diamond Harbour and Governor's Bay, and through the Lyttleton tunnel back to Christchurch city centre.

Above from far left: historic time-keeping; sheep farmer and his flock near Akaroa; expect to see French and English signs in multilingual Akaroa.

Food and Drink 🍴
② BULLY HAYES
57 Beach Road, Akaroa;
tel: 03 304 7533; $$
Bully Hayes was a smuggler in the Pacific in the 1800s, and tales abound of his visits here, no more so than at the café of the same name. Try Bully Hayes' thick and creamy chowder, or the chef's daily choice of tapas for two, all served with salad, breads, avocado and balsamic oil and dukka (a spicy powder).

Cheese Production

Cheese-making has a long history on Banks Peninsula. The earliest documented instances date from around 1844, when settlers used 'chessets' and presses on their farms in its production. The first shipment of cheese to leave the region was lost en route to Wellington, but, by the 1850s, Akaroa's Port Cooper cheese was a hit in Melbourne and sold for 2/6d a pound. It was a thriving industry, as New Zealand's burgeoning gold fields created a strong demand for locally made cheese, and by 1893, cheese factories were dotted all over the peninsula, from Little River to Okains Bay. Today, however, Barry's Bay Cheese is the only factory still operating on the peninsula; cheese-tastings are on offer here, and a large range of cheeses, crackers and local wines are for sale.

HANMER SPRINGS

This tour heads north of Christchurch through the farmland of the Canterbury Plains to the hot-springs resort of Hanmer. Visit Thrillseekers' Canyon, climb Conical Hill, walk the forests and enjoy a soak in the thermal pools.

Hanmer Hikes

There are lots of good short hiking trails around Hanmer, ranging from 20 minutes to two hours. The more energetic will enjoy the Mount Isobel Track, a six-hour return hike through larches and subalpine scrub to the summit of the mountain. The five-and-a-half-hour journey to Dog Stream Waterfall is also popular. Both hikes offer alternative routes on the return.

DISTANCE	266km (165 miles)
TIME	A full day
START	Christchurch
END	Hanmer Springs
POINTS TO NOTE	

This trip can be done as a day tour from Christchurch or linked with the West Coast route on p.86.

The alpine resort township of Hanmer Springs is located in the foothills of the Southern Alps, 135km (84 miles) north of Christchurch. Surrounded by vast tracts of indigenous and native forests in a landscape cut by sometimes me-andering, sometimes roaring rivers, the road to Hanmer is a scenic one.

Driving non-stop to Hanmer Springs will take about two hours, but it's worth taking time en route to enjoy the Waipara Valley vineyards; here, pinot noir, riesling, chardonnay and sauvignon blanc grapes thrive in a warm micro-climate, out of reach of the brisk easterly winds that swirl through the foothills.

TOWARDS WAIPARA

From Cathedral Square, in **Christchurch ❶**, drive north up Colombo Street for six blocks. Turn left on to Bealey Avenue, then turn left on to Sherborne Street (SH74); follow it to Belfast, where it continues as SH1.

Soon after you will cross the wide shingle riverbed of the Waimakariri River, followed by the Ashley and Kowai rivers.

Cafés and Wineries

Approximately 6km (4 miles) beyond **Amberley** – home to the **Nor'Wester Café**, see ⑪①, if you need a pitstop – look out for the regimented rows of grapevines that mark the beginning of the Waipara Valley wine region, around **Waipara ❷**. There are several options if you want to break your journey at this point: try **The Mudhouse Winery**, see ⑪②, 8km (5 miles) north of Amberley, or the **Waipara Springs Winery**, see ⑪③, 4km (2½ miles) north of the Waipara Bridge. Both vineyards are easy to spot on the main drag.

For an even more personal experi-ence, follow the signposts to boutique wineries **Pegasus Bay**, see ⑪④, and **Daniel Schuster Wines**, see ⑪⑤, where you have a good chance of being introduced to the local wines by the passionate winemakers themselves.

WAIKARI

To continue on your way, return to Waipara Junction just beyond the

Waipara Bridge and turn off on to SH7 (signposted to Lewis Pass). Drive through the birch-lined **Weka Pass** (named after a cheeky native New Zealand bird) to **Waikari** ❸, the boarding point for the historic Weka Pass Railway, and nearby Maori Cave Art. Also of interest midway between Waikari and the township of Culverden is the historic Hurunui Hotel (SH7 at Hurunui; tel: 03 314 4207; www.hurunui.co.nz), built of limestone in 1868 to accommodate weary drovers. It has a peaceful garden bar and traditional pub atmosphere.

Look out for St Andrew's Church as

Above from far left: cute kiwi; relaxing at Hanmer Springs; winemaking is big business in this part of the country.

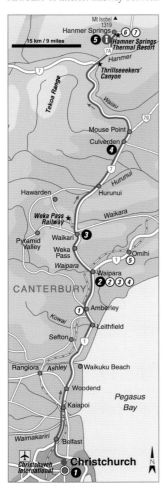

Food and Drink

① NOR'WESTER CAFE
Amberley; tel: 03 314 9411; daily from 10am; $
The perfect place to enjoy southern hospitality and an eclectic menu over a game of dominoes, backgammon or chess – all teamed with a well-matched glass of local wine. Does a good brunch and morning tea, too, for those who are visiting early in the day.

② THE MUDHOUSE WINERY
780 Glasnevin Road, Waipara; tel: 03 314 6900; daily 9am–5pm; $$–$$$
Fresh New Zealand cuisine teamed with a selection of the vineyard's wines.

③ WAIPARA SPRINGS WINERY
409 Omihi Road/SH1, Waipara; tel: 03 314 6777; www.waiparasprings.co.nz; $$
Located 4km (2½ miles) north of the Waipara Bridge this winery offers a range of set lunches, platters, plus light bites, all accompanied by the house wines. Good vegetarian choices too.

④ PEGASUS BAY WINERY
Stockgrove Road, Waipara; tel: 03 314 6869; $$
This family-owned operation is one of New Zealand's finest boutique wineries. Its sauvignon semillon, riesling, chardonnay, pinot noir and cabernet/merlot can be sampled at the tasting bar or matched to the menu, which uses local ingredients. Chargrilled Hereford beef fillet is offered with the vineyard's premium pinot noir; brie de Meaux tart is the food of choice for Pegasus Bay Chardonnay. Alternatively there's the Pegasus Bay platters, which come piled high and are great for sharing. Recommended.

⑤ DAVID SCHUSTER WINES
Omihi Hills Vineyard, 192 Reeces Road, Omihi; Waipara; tel: 03 314 5901; www.danielschusterwines.com; daily 10am–5pm; $$
Established in 1986 this small family-owned producer just east of Omihi has a tasting room, where you can sample its wines. You can also look into the cellar and admire the views of the valley.

Above from left: Hanmer Springs; the lakeside Church of the Good Shepherd.

Below: hands-on experience of Maori crafts, using the *harakeke* (flax) plant.

Historic Springs

The Maori knew of Hanmer Springs long before Europeans came on the scene. Their legends speak of Tamatea, whose canoe was wrecked off the Otago coast. To save his party from freezing he called upon the mountains of Tongariro and Ngauruhoe in the north for help. They sent flames down the Whanganui River and over to Nelson, where they rose in the air and landed in Hanmer Springs.

you drive (still on SH7) through **Culverden 4**, once a main rail terminus but now a small town of fewer than 500 people, and, at the Waiau River, anglers fishing for salmon and trout.

HANMER SPRINGS

About 126km (78 miles) from Christchurch is the SH7A turn off to **Hanmer Springs 5**. Make the turn, then look for the car park 200m (219yds) ahead on your right. Park here and go for a walk to see dramatic views of **Thrillseekers' Canyon**. A stroll leads to the 140-year-old single-lane **Waiau Ferry Bridge**, which still has its original steelwork intact; it quickly becomes clear how this gorge got its name. Bungy-jumpers leap from here into the fast-flowing Waiau River; jet-boat rides and whitewater rafting trips are on offer too. Join in or soak up the adrenalin-charged atmosphere, then continue to Hanmer, about 8km (5 miles) up the road.

As you enter town, make a stop at the **Hurunui i-SITE Visitor Centre** (42 Amuri Avenue West; tel: 0800 442 663; www.hurunui.com; daily 9.30am–5pm), adjacent to the Hanmer Springs Thermal Reserve's hot pools.

Hikers should walk the half-hour **Zig-Zag Track** up Conical Hill, just behind the township. From here there are fine views over the Hanmer Basin. Walk up Conical Hill Road to reach the start of the track, calling in at **Mumbles**, see ⑪⑥, if you need refreshment.

Hot Springs

As a relaxing alternative, or as a wind-down after some of the more energetic local activities, soak in the hot pools at **Hanmer Springs Thermal Resort & Spa** (Amuri Avenue; tel: 03 315 7511; www.hanmersprings.co.nz; daily 10am–9pm; charge), just east of the visitor information centre.

The springs were first used by ancient Maori, stopping en route to the West Coast to collect *pounamu* (jade). Although they feature in ancient Maori legends, the pools were only 'discovered' by Europeans in 1859, and further development was hindered by the inaccessibility of the region. The first iron bathing shed was erected in 1879, and in post-war years the recuperative powers of the springs were used by the nearby Queen Mary Hospital to assist in the recovery of soldiers returning from the war. There are now seven open-air thermal pools, three sulphur pools and four private pools, plus therapeutic massage or beauty treatment.

When you are feeling suitably refreshed, consider a bite to eat at the **Gardenhouse Café**, see ⑪⑦, then either retrace your way to Christchurch, or continue through the beech-covered slopes of the Lewis Pass to link up with the West Coast tour *(see p.86)*.

Food and Drink 🍴

⑥ MUMBLES CAFÉ

6 Conical Hill Road, Hanmer Springs; tel: 03 315 7124; $
Unpretentious home-cooked food served by friendly locals.

⑦ GARDENHOUSE CAFÉ

Amuri Avenue, Hanmer Springs; tel: 03 315 7511; $
Located within the Hanmer Springs Thermal Resort complex, so recommended for its convenience above all else. Good for kids.

CHRISTCHURCH TO QUEENSTOWN

A multi-day trip from Christchurch to Queenstown via Aoraki/Mount Cook, New Zealand's highest mountain. Overnight at Mount Cook Village, enjoy a flight above the Tasman Glacier and Southern Alps, then continue through the plains of the Mackenzie Country hinterland to Queenstown.

From **Christchurch ❶**, head south on SH1, travelling on the long straights of the plains of South Canterbury, a colourful patchwork of fields flanked by the dramatic peaks of the Southern Alps, crossing New Zealand's longest bridge over the Rakaia River.

Drive through **Ashburton**, then take the turn-off on to SH79 shortly after crossing the Rangitata River, where kayaks and whitewater rafts negotiate the wilder stretches of water.

GERALDINE

Geraldine ❷, on the banks of the Waihi River, is a good place to stop and stretch your legs. Popular with artisans, it's a hive of creativity. You can tempt your tastebuds on Talbot Street, too, either at Talbot Forest Cheese (76 Talbot Street; tel: 03 693 1111), Barker Fruit Processors (76 Talbot Street; tel: 03 693 9727), Chocolate Fellmann (10 Talbot Street; tel: 03 693 9982; *see p.84*) or the **Verde Café**, see ⓐⓘ. At the Giant Jersey (10 Wilson Street; tel: 03 693 9820; www.giantjersey.co.nz), gorgeously soft perendale, mohair and merino wools are crafted into stylish made-to-measure garments.

DISTANCE 491km (305 miles)
TIME Two to three days
START Christchurch
END Queenstown
POINTS TO NOTE
You will need a car for this tour; for details of car-hire firms, *see p.111.* The drive from Christchurch to Aoraki/Mount Cook covers 331km (206 miles) and will take about five hours. From Aoraki/Mount Cook it is 262km (163 miles) to Queenstown; about another four hours on the road. The scenery, however, more than compensates.

FAIRLIE

Return to your vehicle and continue on SH79 to **Fairlie ❸**, the gateway to the Mackenzie Country, where huge oak trees provide shady relief for picnickers on the main street.

Flying Alternative
If you don't have time to drive but would still like to see the glaciers and peaks of the Southern Alps and Aoraki/Mount Cook, the direct Air New Zealand flight from Christchurch to Queenstown offers spectacular views, weather permitting. Also note that depending on what time you plan to arrive, it's best to book ahead for a ski-plane flight to the glaciers and Aoraki Mount Cook with Mount Cook Ski Planes *(see p.85).*

Food and Drink 🍴
① VERDE CAFÉ
45 Talbot Street, Geraldine; tel: 03 693 9616; $
Set behind a white picket fence close to the river, this is a great coffee stop with a fine selection of sweet treats.

Above from left:
view of Aoraki/Mount
Cook from Lake
Pukaki; Church of
the Good Shepherd,
Lake Tekapo; statue
of Sir Edmund Hillary;
the Tasman Glacier.

For Chocoholics
Chocolate Fellmann
on the main street
of Geraldine *(see
p.83)* is a chocolate-
lover's paradise,
offering a fine
selection of delectable
goodies. Swiss-born
patissier/confiseur/
chocolatier René
Fellmann does not
believe in adding
compounds and
uses only the best
of ingredients. His
range includes
pralines, gateaux,
chocolate mice
and a Kiwi classic –
chocolate 'fish', a
chocolate-covered,
fish-shaped
marshmallow treat.

A quick stroll round town takes in
highlights such as the Heritage
Museum. For a place to stop, there's
the **Old Library Café**, see ⑪②.

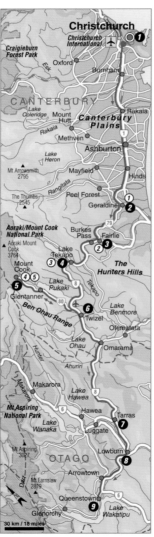

LAKE TEKAPO

You now begin the steep ascent past
the colonial homesteads of Burkes
Pass, and on through the Mackenzie
Country's striking vast plains to the
township of **Lake Tekapo** ❹. The historic **Church of the Good Shepherd**,
built from locally gathered stones
as a memorial to the pioneers of
the Mackenzie Country, is a favourite
photo stop and offers grandstand views
of the lake, which is fed by glacier-melt
from the Alps. A solitary bronze
sheepdog stands guard nearby, in
honour of all high-country mustering
dogs. **Pepe's Pizza & Pasta**, see ⑪③,
is a good choice for a bite here.

Stop by the lake for a stretch and –
season permitting – consider spending
an hour skating at Tekapo's all-new
lakeside **Winter Park** (6 Lakeside
Drive; tel: 03 680 6550; www.winter
park.co.nz; open daily; charge), before
continuing on to **Lake Pukaki** to
enjoy the dramatic views of **Mount
Cook** across its shimmering waters.

MOUNT COOK VILLAGE

Further on, take the turn-off into SH80
for the stunning 55-km (34-mile) drive
beneath Ben Ohau's textured peaks to
Glentanner, where the lake meets glacial river rubble. From here a vast valley
of earthy tones and charcoal-coloured
scree slopes leads to **Mount Cook Village** ❺. If you love the great outdoors,
there's lots to do here, and you may
want to stay for several days *(see p.117)*.
For dining options, see ⑪④–⑤.

Here, you are within the Aoraki/ Mount Cook National Park, and the local visitor centre has up-to-date information on the park's geology, climate, flora and fauna. There are lots of walks from the village, ranging from ten minutes to four hours in length. A must-do is the 30-minute hike to the Tasman Glacier viewpoint, which provides first-class views. Alternatively, join a Glacier Explorers boat adventure to see where the glacier yields its icemelt to the glacier lake, before being washed away downstream.

Aoraki/Mount Cook

The **Aoraki/Mount Cook** is New Zealand's highest mountain, at 3,764m (12,348ft). From the small **airport** on SH80 you can fly with Mount Cook Ski Planes (tel: 03 435 1026; www.ski planes.co.nz; daily, depart on the half-hour; charge) to view some of the most awe-inspiring scenery in New Zealand. Land at the head of the Tasman Glacier – no ice axes or crampons required – or consider heli-skiing or Alpine Guides' 'Ski the Tasman' package (Sir Edmund Hillary Centre, Hermitage Hotel; tel: 03 435 1834; www.alpine guides.co.nz; daily) to get up close and personal with the gentle bowls, open snowfields, towering seracs and icefalls of the national park.

BACK TO QUEENSTOWN

To return to Queenstown, go back to SH80 and drive south on SH8 past **Twizel ❻** and **Tarras ❼**. After **Low-burn ❽**, take the turn-off right for SH6 and continue into **Queenstown ❾**.

Sir Edmund Hillary
Edmund Percival Hillary was born in Auckland in 1919. On 29 May 1953, he and Nepalese Sherpa mountaineer Tenzing Norgay became the first climbers known to have reached Mount Everest's summit, on a British expedition led by John Hunt. In his later years, Hillary devoted much of his time to humanitarian and conservation work and is respected as much in his native New Zealand for this as for his conquest of Everest. He died in Auckland in 2008. He graces the country's $5 bill.

Food and Drink

② OLD LIBRARY CAFÉ
7 Allandale Road, Fairlie; tel: 03 685 8999; $$
Housed in the atmospheric old town library, this place has an all-day menu. Highlights include locally sourced food, notably the excellent lamb and the delectable, locally sourced Mount Cook salmon.

③ PEPE'S PIZZA & PASTA
Main Street, Tekapo; tel: 03 680 6677; $$
In a niche of its own among the many fine-dining establishments along Tekapo's ridge, Pepe's offers great value for money, an ambient atmosphere with fireside dining and a cosy bar, and incredibly good pizza. Favourites include the Smoked Salmon Siesta – thin-crust pizza topped with smoked Mount Cook salmon, onion, zucchini and wasabi sauce; and Vinnie's Venison, topped with roast venison, kumara, and pumpkin served with lashings of spiced plum sauce.

④ PANORAMA RESTAURANT
The Hermitage Hotel, Mount Cook Village; tel: 03 435 1809; $$–$$$
Executive chef Franz Blum uses the freshest produce, sourced locally and from around New Zealand to prepare superb cuisine. Incredible views over the mountains. The hotel *(see p.117)* also houses the Snowline Bar.

⑤ CHAMOIS BAR
Mount Cook Village; tel: 03 435 1809; $
This is the locals' favourite place to enjoy a hearty, home-style pub meal of mammoth proportions.

ARTHUR'S PASS AND THE WEST COAST

This three-day driving tour provides an alternative route from Christ-church to Queenstown, travelling from the Pacific Coast, through Arthur's Pass in the Southern Alps, to the Tasman Sea. The scenery is breathtaking all the way to Franz Josef and Fox glaciers, and beyond.

Jade Route

Maori first used Arthur's Pass on journeys to gather precious *pounamu* (jade) on the West Coast. Settlers later opened a road across the Canterbury Plains, up Porters Pass and into the Waimakariri Basin, which was used to carry dray-loads of wool to Christchurch from the inland sheep stations. When gold was discovered on the West Coast, the provincial government provided funds to extend the road through Arthur's Pass to the goldfields. One thousand men were employed, and the road was built in less than a year.

DISTANCE 754km (468 miles)
TIME Three days
START Christchurch
END Queenstown
POINTS TO NOTE
You will need a car for this tour; for details of car hire, *see p.111.* Bring warm clothes, sensible shoes and a torch for the cave visit detailed below.

The 260-km (160-mile) route over the scenic Arthur's Pass to Hokitika on the West Coast provides one of the country's great geographical contrasts. This alpine highway climbs through a visual feast of mirrored lakes, caves and rock formations, ridges and valleys, wide shingle riverbeds and deep gorges.

CHRISTCHURCH TO LAKE LYNDON

From Cathedral Square in **Christchurch ❶**, head south on Colombo Street; follow the road for three blocks and turn right on to Tuam Street. Continue to Christchurch Hospital and then drive into Hagley Park on Riccarton Avenue. Follow this all the way through the suburb of Riccarton, then veer right on to Yaldhurst Road, following the signposts for Arthur's Pass on to SH73.

This route takes you through the town of **Darfield ❷**, where **Terrace**, see ⑪①, is an option if you're hungry. From Darfield, continue on towards **Sheffield** and then **Springfield**, 70km (43½ miles) from Christchurch. SH73 climbs swiftly beyond Springfield into the foothills of the Southern Alps. At the same time, the scenery becomes increasingly dramatic.

Follow the road over **Porter's Pass** (923m/3028ft), which passes **Lake Lyndon** and the turn-off to Porter's Pass skifield, before you go past Kura Tawhiti (Castle Hill Reserve). **Cave Stream Scenic Reserve** is about 6km (4 miles) further on, and has a car park with good views of the basin area.

Cave Visit

Unless you suffer from claustrophobia, spend an hour exploring the 362-m (1,188-ft) limestone cave here, with its flowing stream and Maori cave art. You will need warm clothes, a torch with spare batteries, and a change of clothes for when you exit the cave.

ARTHUR'S PASS VILLAGE

SH73 passes **Lake Pearson** (pull into the rest area on the right for access to this lake), **Lake Grassmere** and **Lake Sarah**, before meeting up with the braided Waimakariri River. About 40km (25 miles) beyond Castle Hill is the **Bealey Hotel ❸**, see ⓦ② and *p.117*, built when the road opened in 1866 to accommodate Cobb and Co. passengers on the three-day stage-coach journey to the West Coast. It is still an option if you want to stay overnight.

Another 10km (6 miles) and you will arrive in **Arthur's Pass Village ❹**, set in a bush-covered river valley among the mountains in the Arthur's Pass National Park. On the left heading into the village, there is a **visitor centre** (daily 8am–5pm; tel: 03 318 9211) with displays on local flora and fauna, and a video clip recalling the story of the first pass crossing. There is also information on a variety of walks in the area. Time permitting, you could hike the 2-km (1¼-mile) track known as **Devil's Punch Bowl**, which leads to the base of a 131-m (430-ft) waterfall.

Above from far left: West Coast beach; helicopter flights over Aoraki Mount Cook offer spectacular views.

Above: views of Shantytown *(see p88)*.

Food and Drink 🍴

① **TERRACE CAFÉ & BAR**
20 Main South Terrace, Darfield; 03 318 7303; $-$$
Seasonal menu featuring locally reared meat (Canterbury lamb) and local salmon.

② **BEALEY HOTEL**
SH73, Arthur's Pass; tel: 03 318 9277; $
Hearty pub fare served in a magnificent mountain setting. *See also p.117.*

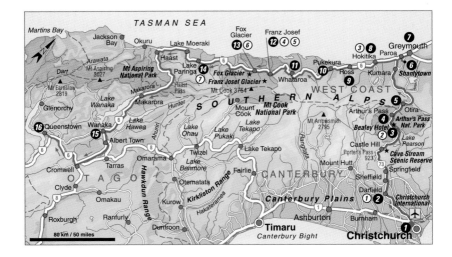

OTIRA

Leaving the village, the road climbs steeply for 4km (2½ miles) to the pass (912m/2,992ft), where you can pull into a signposted lookout on the right for glorious views and the company of a cheeky, green native kea (parrot).

From here the road descends steeply via the modern Otira Viaduct into the old railway township of **Otira ❺**. You are now on the West Coast – known in New Zealand as the Wild West Coast or sometimes the Wet Coast; the hardy locals are proud of the pristine condition of their precious rainforests, and the climate that keeps them that way.

Below: rugged West Coast beach.

SHANTYTOWN

While Maori journeyed to the West Coast for *pounamu* (jade), European settlers came for gold. A good way to experience those days of old is at **Shantytown ❻** (tel: 0800 742 689; www.shantytown.co.nz; daily 8.30am–5pm; charge). To get there, follow SH73 through the town of **Kumara** and then on to Kumara Junction. At the junction, head north on SH6, following the signs to Greymouth, turning off at **Paroa**, and follow the signs to Shantytown.

Highlights

This replica West Coast settlement has more than 30 historic buildings to see, including a sawmill, stables, bank, hotel, barber's shop, miners' hall, printing works and blacksmith. You can take a ride on a steam train (departs hourly throughout the day), including the 25-tonne *Kaitangata*, built in 1897 on tracks that follow the route of an old sawmill tramline. Like many of the first bush tramways in New Zealand, this historic route was originally wooden-railed and worked by horses. You can also try your hand at panning for alluvial gold here.

Food and Drink 🍴

③ **STUMPERS CAFÉ**
2 Weld Street, Hokitika; 03 755 6154; $$
Stumpers offers stylish home-made cuisine as well as local delicacies, including West Coast whitebait, beer-battered blue cod, venison and rack of lamb.

GREYMOUTH

It's another 10km (6 miles) north into **Greymouth ❼**, where highlights include the **Jade Boulder Gallery**, a museum that tells the story of this semi-precious stone, and **Monteith's Brewery** (60 Herbert Street; tel: 03 768 4149; www.monteiths.co.nz; charge), a classic West Coast icon, offering tours of the plant followed by a tasting.

HOKITIKA

If you're planning to stay overnight on this part of the coast, it's worth backtracking on SH6 and continuing 40km (25 miles) south to **Hokitika ❽**, as the distances to other attractions further south make this the perfect night stop. For details of hotels, *see p.118*. There isn't much to do in this town in the evenings, except catch a movie at the Regent cinema (15 Weld Street) or admire glow-worms in the signposted dell 1km (⅔ mile) north on SH6. Alternatively, dine at **Stumpers**, see ⑪③.

West Coast Historical Museum
In the morning visit the **West Coast Historical Museum** (tel: 03 755 6898; www.nzmuseums.co.nz; summer daily 9.30am–5pm, winter Mon–Fri 9.30am–5pm, Sat–Sun 10am–2pm; charge), accessed via the Hokitika Visitor Centre (Carnegie Building, corner of Tancred and Hamilton streets; tel: 03 755 6166).

The museum mounts an audio-visual show telling the story of the West Coast gold rushes. In 1864, Hokitika grew almost overnight into a major commercial area and one of New Zealand's busiest ports, despite the treacherous sandbar that claimed 32 ships between 1865 and 1867. The kumara rush marked the end of a golden age, and most fortune-seekers drifted off to try their luck elsewhere.

Pick up the *Hokitika Heritage Trail* leaflet at the museum and take a walk around town, combining your tour with an exploration of the jade galleries and studios of Hokitika's many artisans, who include glassblowers, jewellers, woodturners and potters.

JOURNEY TO THE GLACIERS

There is a lot of driving to do today, so don't linger for too long in Hokitika. Fill up with petrol (gas), make sure you've got some cash to hand because there are no banks until you get to Wanaka or Queenstown, and head south on SH6 to the glaciers 148km (92 miles) further down the coast.

Ross
On the way you will pass through the town of **Ross ❾**, where the largest gold nugget in New Zealand was unearthed in 1909. It weighed 3.6kg (7.9lb) and was presented to King George V as a coronation present. The **Ross Visitor Centre** (4 Aylmer Street; tel: 03 755 4033; daily 9am–4.30pm; charge) provides information on the area's history.

Pukekura
Drive another 25km (15½ miles) further south and watch out for the giant

Above from far left: the TranzAlpine Express Train en route to Greymouth; West Coast forest; the coast in this area is famous for its whitebait (the season runs Sept–Nov).

West Coast Rocks Punakaiki has 'pancake rocks' (limestone formations that look like towers of giant flapjacks) and surf blowholes.

Hiking the Glacier
Franz Josef Glacier
Guides (SH6, Franz
Josef; tel: 0800 484
337; www.franzjosef
glacier.com) provide
access to a unique
hiking experience:
tramping on Franz
Josef, the world's
steepest and fastest-
flowing commercially
guided glacier.
Specially designed
'Ice Talonz' are
strapped on over your
boots. At first the
Talonz feel ungainly,
but, before long,
your speed picks up,
and you should be
walking on the glacier
like a pro.

sandfly sculpture that marks the small settlement of **Pukekura ⑩**. Stop off at the **Bushman's Museum and Bushman's Centre** (tel: 03 755 4144; daily 9am–5pm; charge) for an entertaining insight into West Coast life.

Towards Whataroa

Continue another 4km (2½ miles) past the serene shores of trout-filled **Lake Ianthe**, and on though **Harihari** to **Whataroa ⑪**, the renowned breeding grounds of the graceful and rare *kotuku*, or white heron. Access to its breeding grounds is restricted to group trips run by White Heron Sanctuary Tours (tel: 03 753 4120; www.whiteherontours.co. nz; charge). *See also margin opposite.*

FRANZ JOSEF VILLAGE AND GLACIER

Shortly after driving past **Lake Mapourika** (famous for its trout and salmon), you will arrive at the village of **Franz Josef ⑫**, home of the magnificent **Franz Josef Glacier**. Your first stop should be the **visitor centre** (SH6; tel: 03 752 0796; daily 8.30am–6pm), for maps and further information. For half- and full-day guided tours walking on the ice of Franz Josef Glacier, contact Franz Josef Glacier Guides (tel: 03 752 0763; www.franz josefglacier.co.nz). There are also scenic plane rides and helicopter flights to Franz Josef and/or Fox glaciers, as well as scenic flights to Aoraki/Mount Cook.

If you prefer to take a look at the glacier on your own, drive over the **Waiho River** and turn right, driving a further 5km (3 miles) into the car park. From here a 90-minute walk along a 4-km (2½-mile) trail from the car park will take you face to face with this giant river of ice. However, without crampons or ice talons (provided on the

Food and Drink 🍴

④ CHEEKY KEA
Main Road, Franz Josef Village; tel: 03 752 0139; $
Affordable family fare including roast meals and country-fried chicken and chips.

⑤ BLUE ICE
SH6, Franz Josef Village; tel: 03 752 0707; $$
Popular with locals and visitors alike this great café/restaurant offers an à-la-carte menu of Pacific Rim and classic New Zealand dishes plus staples such as pizza.

⑥ CAFÉ NEVE
Main Road, Fox Glacier; tel: 03 751 0100; $$
A friendly café/restaurant serving a variety of cuisine, including award-winning beef and lamb, seafood, venison and gourmet pizza.

⑦ SOUTH WESTLAND SALMON
SH6, Paringa; tel: 03 751 0837; $–$$
Sample freshly hooked farmed salmon and hot smoked salmon at this farm café.

tour), the glacier itself is too slippery and dangerous to explore on foot.

There's a range of accommodation available in Franz Josef; for details, *see p.119*. Good places to eat in the village include **Cheeky Kea**, see ⑪④, and **Blue Ice**, see ⑪⑤.

FOX GLACIER VILLAGE AND GLACIER

The village of **Fox Glacier** ⑬, 25km (15½ miles) to the south, is smaller than Franz Josef. The visitor centre (on the right as you enter town) has an extremely informative display on the history, geology and ecology of the glacier region. **Café Neve**, see ⑪⑥, is an option for refreshment.

To get to the glacier itself, drive through the town and turn left on to Glacier Road. You'll reach a car park after 6km (4 miles), and from there it is a 30-minute walk to the face of the glacier. If you prefer a guided tour, book direct with Alpine Guides (tel: 03 751 0825; www.foxguides.co.nz). Time and weather permitting, take a short detour to Lake Matheson from town, following the signs off SH6 to see views of the summit of Aoraki/ Mount Cook and Fox Glacier mirrored in the waters of the lake.

If you choose to stay overnight in Fox Glacier, *see p.119* for hotels.

PARINGA

From Fox Glacier, continue south on SH6 through Kahikatea Forest past **Lake Paringa** ⑭ (look out for the excellent **South Westland Salmon**, see ⑪⑦, if you want to stop on the way) and Lake Moeraki.

BACK TO QUEENSTOWN

To reach Queenstown there is a lot of distance to cover (267km/166 miles to Wanaka and 338km/210 miles to Queenstown), driving through the magnificent Haast Pass in the **Mount Aspiring National Park**. Keep on SH6 all the way. Here towering peaks surround vast open valleys and lofty waterfalls plunge from steep green cliffs. Make a stop at the spectacular 'Gates of Haast' bridge before continuing on to **Wanaka** ⑮, a pleasant town with an attractive lake and good watersports facilities. From here continue on SH6 to **Queenstown** ⑯.

Above from far left: view into an ice cave on the Franz Josef Glacier; the top of the Franz Josef Glacier; alpine sign.

Heron Colony
White Heron Sanctuary Tours provide access to New Zealand's only nesting colony of the white heron via jet-boat, which travels down the Waitangitaona and Waitangiroto rivers, through towering kahikatea forest to a small jetty. From there, boardwalks lead past a series of predator traps and through native kotukutuku, makomako and miro trees to a screened viewing platform. The first herons arrive at these breeding grounds in early September, and, after courtship, nest high above the water. From the viewing platform you can spy on their nests and watch them feed their chicks with food from the nearby Okarito Lagoon (SH6, Whataroa; tel: 0800 523 456; www.white herontours.co.nz).

Left: Aoraki/ Mount Cook and Lake Pukaki.

QUEENSTOWN

It's easy to see why Queenstown is unashamedly a tourist town, given its location in an area of spectacular natural beauty. There is a huge range of leisure activities on offer and great shopping. This tour, encompassing gondola rides, bungy-jumping and jet-boat rides, covers its highlights.

DISTANCE 14km (8 miles)

TIME A full day

START Queenstown i-SITE Visitor Centre

END Queenstown Gardens

POINTS TO NOTE

A number of activities are recommended as part of this tour. Reserve in advance, if there is an activity you are particularly keen to do.

Maori History

In the early days Central Otago was the great divide that the Maori had to cross in order to access the greenstone, or *pounamu*, from the mountains of the West Coast. The stone was often used to make *tiki*, Polynesian amulets in the shape of a human figure, believed to be endowed with *mana* or power.

Resting on the shore of Lake Wakatipu, with mountains looming all around and valleys cut deep by swift-flowing rivers, Queenstown in Central Otago is the quintessential year-round holiday resort. It has grown from a sleepy lakeside town into a sophisticated all-year tourist attraction. Within a radius of only a few kilometres, the ingenuity and mechanical wizardry of New Zealanders have combined with the stunning landscape to provide an unrivalled range of adventure activities. Little wonder, then, that the city is often dubbed the 'Adventure Capital of the World'.

SKYLINE GONDOLA

Begin your day at the **Queenstown i-SITE Visitor Centre ❶** (Clocktower Building, corner Shotover and Camp streets; tel: 03 442 4100; www.queenstown-vacation.com; daily 7.30am–6.30pm; free). Here you can pick up maps and brochures outlining the vast range of outdoor pursuits available in Queenstown. For a great breakfast nearby, head to **Joe's Garage**, see ⑪①, a short walk down Camp Street.

Head northwest up Camp Street, then take the first left into Isle Street and the first right into Brecon Street, home both to **Bezu**, see ⑪②, and the **Skyline Gondola ❷** (tel: 03 441 0101; www.skyline.co.nz; daily 9am–late; charge). The gondola rises some 450m (1,476ft) up Bob's Peak to a magnificent view of Queenstown, Lake Wakatipu and The Remarkables mountain range. At the top there's a restaurant, café, gift shop and an outdoor viewing deck.

A walking track leads to the base for an activity that has become a New Zealand icon – bungy-jumping. This particular operation is called The Ledge and is run by bungy pioneer A.J. Hackett (tel: 03 442 7100; www.bungy.co.nz; daily: summer noon–7pm, winter 3–9pm). It offers spectacular views of Queenstown – if you manage to keep your eyes open – as you take the plunge.

Speed demons can ride the chairlifts to a higher elevation and take the **Luge** (daily, weather dependent; charge), a thrilling ride down the mountainside.

CADDYSHACK CITY

Returning on the gondola to Brecon Street, you have the opportunity to visit **Caddyshack City ❸** (tel: 03 442 6642; daily 10am–6pm; charge), an elaborate mini-golf centre, and the Kiwi Birdlife Park (Brecon Street; tel: 03 442 8059; daily; charge), an ideal place to spot kiwis of the feathered kind, if you haven't already.

STEAMER WHARF

Back on Brecon Street, turn right at Shotover Street and follow the road around to the **Steamer Wharf Village**

❹, where there are shops and restaurants, including the lakefront **19th Restaurant**, see ⑪③.

The wharf is also home to a variety of vessels, but none so distinctive as the TSS *Earnslaw (see p.94)*, which was launched in 1912 and is affectionately known to locals as 'The Lady of the Lake'. The coal-fired boilers belch the Earnslaw's trademark black smoke as she carries passengers on sightseeing tours. Book your cruise tickets with Real Journeys (Steamer Wharf; tel: 03 442 7500; www.realjourneys.co.nz; daily, departures every two hours 10am–8pm; charge) for the 2pm excursion to Walter Peak *(see p.94)*.

Above from far left:
Lake Wakatipu; bungy jumping at Bob's Peak; Kawarau Suspension Bridge; the Remarkables.

Lord of the Rings
The Queenstown region was the location for numerous scenes in the *Lord of the Rings* movies. Many are, however, inaccessible without a helicopter ride. Taking one of several 'Rings' tours gets over this problem: see www.trilogytrail.com for details.

Food and Drink 🍴

① JOE'S GARAGE
7 Arrow Lane; tel: 03 442 5282; $$
With its strong coffee focus, Joe's Garage has built up street cred with its breakfast/brunch menu.

② BEZU
2nd floor, Sofitel, Brecon Street; tel: 03 409 2302; $–$$$
Brunch, lunch and dinner are on offer at this distinctively European-style bar/café.

③ 19TH RESTAURANT
Steamer Wharf; tel: 03 442 4006; $$
This informal café/bar is right on the lake – any further and you'd get wet – and the perfect place to relax on a hot day. Menu of light café classics.

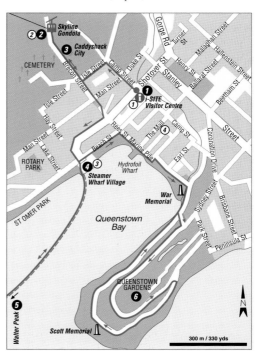

Above from left:
cruising on the
Earnslaw; jet-boat
on the Shotover river;
golden nuggets –
the reason for Arrow-
town's development
in the 19th century;
the Remarkables and
Lake Wakatipu.

Whitewater Rafting

The rugged beauty
and unspoiled
grandeur of the
upper reaches of the
Shotover River also
provide the setting for
extreme whitewater-
rafting excitement;
while the slightly
tamer Kawarau
River provides an
exhilarating ride and
a great introduction
to whitewater rafting
for first-time rafters.
There are four rapids
to negotiate, including
the final (unforgettable)
400-m (1,312-ft) Dog
Leg rapid. Kawarau
rafters will gain an
unusual perspective
of bungy-jumpers
plummeting from
the Kawarau
Suspension Bridge.

SHOTOVER JET-BOAT RIDE

Before then, though, there's an option to fit in some more action in the form of a jet-boat ride. Shotover Jets (Gorge Road, Arthur's Point; tel: 03 442 8570; www.shotoverjet.co.nz; daily, boats depart every 15 mins) operate on the Shotover River, 6km (4 miles) from town. A courtesy bus departs from the information centre (corner Shotover and Camp streets), taking the adventurous out to the jetty near Arthur's Point every 15 minutes. The jet-boat drivers are highly skilled, and their sense of humour can be gauged by the smiles on their faces as they spin you within inches of overhanging rocks. Although the boat ride only takes 30 minutes, add another hour for the ride to the river and back.

CAVELL MALL

On your return you may want to get your 'land legs' back by wandering around the waterfront and **Cavell Mall** area. Although much of Queenstown's architecture is contemporary, some of its attractive original buildings are still standing, including the former Eichardts' pub (1871) on Marine Parade – now a lodge and stylish bar

– and the courthouse and library buildings, built in 1876, at the corner of Ballarat and Stanley streets.

Winnie's, see ⑪④, is a good pitstop in this area, if you are hungry.

EARNSLAW CRUISE

As 2pm draws near, make your way back to the wharf for your three-hour cruise on the TSS *Earnslaw* to **Walter Peak ⑤**. On the western shore of the lake, Walter Peak is the original homestead of one of New Zealand's most famous sheep and cattle stations. The cruise across takes about 40 minutes, leaving you plenty of time to enjoy the gardens surrounding the homestead as well as watch a sheep-shearing demonstration and admire the herd of Scottish Highland cattle.

QUEENSTOWN GARDENS

Return to Queenstown and round the day off with a late-afternoon stroll around **Queenstown Gardens ⑥** (free) on the far side of Queenstown Bay. To get there, walk around past the jetty and along Marine Parade to the War Memorial, on a tree-lined promenade just behind the beachfront. Beyond it, a pathway leads into the gardens where you can wander at your leisure. Look out for the dramatic memorial to Antarctic explorer Robert Falcon Scott.

Circling back, you will gain views of Kelvin Heights, then of Walter Peak. This is a great place to watch the sunset, before returning along the beachfront and walking back into town.

Food and Drink 🍴

④ WINNIE'S

7–9 The Mall; tel: 03 442 8635; $

Winnie's is a lively bar and restaurant with a reputation for delicious gourmet pizza and pasta. That, plus the happy hours, pool tables and live music, make it popular with backpackers.

ARROWTOWN

This tour is a drive over the Shotover Gorge, through Arthur's Point and up to Coronet Peak for a panoramic view of the Wakatipu Basin, before ascending to picturesque historic Arrowtown, a former gold-mining town.

A trip to Arrowtown, 21km (13 miles) from Queenstown, is a journey into the region's past. Situated in a quiet, leafy gully, the town played a prominent role in the gold-rush days of the 1860s, attracting fortune-seekers from around the world. As the gold diminished, so did Arrowtown's importance. It did not, however, go the way of desolation of so many other gold-mining settlements in the vicinity, slipping instead into a quieter way of life and revelling in its beautiful location.

QUEENSTOWN TO CORONET PEAK

In **Queenstown** ❶, turn left at the northern end of Shotover Street into Gorge Road. Continue for around 6km (4 miles), travelling past **Arthur's Point Tavern**. Some 500m (547yds) further on is the historic **Edith Cavell Bridge** *(see right)*, which spans the Shotover River. Continue on the same route (it becomes Malaghans Road), passing Arthur's Point Camp Ground on your right and the **Shotover Stables** (Domain Road; tel: 03 442 7486; www.shotoverstables.net; daily 9.30am, 1.30pm, 3.30pm; charge) on your left, where 90-minute horse rides are available for beginners through to advanced riders.

DISTANCE 83km (51 miles)
TIME A half-day
START/END Queenstown
POINTS TO NOTE
You will need a car for this tour; for details of car hire, *see p.111.* This trip includes a stop at a vineyard; note the local rules on drink/driving *(see p.65).*

Slow down as you pass **Nugget Point** (146 Arthur's Point Road; tel: 03 441 0288; www.nuggetpoint.co.nz), a luxury lodge overlooking the Shotover River, because just beyond on the left is the turn-off to **Coronet Peak** and **Skippers Canyon**. The latter is off-limits to most rental cars owing to its treacherous nature. Should you wish to explore, Nomad Safaris (tel: 03 442 6699; www.nomadsafaris.co.nz; daily 8.30am, 1.30pm; charge) offer guided tours.

However, Coronet Peak, a top-class ski-field in the winter, is easily accessible with a fully sealed mountain road of around 20km (12½ miles); allow 40 minutes for the return trip. Here, every year in early July, Coronet Peak comes alive during the **Queenstown Winter Festival** (tel: 03 441 2453; www.winterfestival.co.nz; charge). Celebrity skiers, sheepdog trials, night skiing and all-night partying signal the

Edith Cavell
Born in 1865 to a clergyman and his wife in Norfolk, England, Cavell is known for her extraordinary achievements as a nurse and humanitarian. A nurse during World War I, she helped hundreds of Allied soldiers to escape from occupied Belgium to the neutral Netherlands. She was arrested by in 1915 and executed on 12 October. The Edith Cavell Bridge over the Shotover River is one of many memorials named in her honour.

Prime Skiing
In the winter, the Southern Lakes region of the South Island is transformed into a magical wonderland, with perfect powder snow covering the slopes of the surrounding mountain ranges. There are four ski-fields within easy access of Queenstown and Wanaka: Coronet Peak, Cardrona, Treble Cone and the Remarkables.

Dorothy Browns

Arrowtown is home to one of New Zealand's quirkiest movie houses, Dorothy Browns Cinema, Bar and Bookshop (tel: 64 3 442 1968; www. dorothybrowns.com) on Buckingham Street. This charming boutique cinema shows arthouse films (check online for the schedule) and has unusually large, comfortable seating, an open fire and a bar. It is apparently named after a turn-of-the-century photographer, who lived with one of the Chinese workers from the local gold-mining community.

start of the ski season in the region. But no matter the season, it is a superb place to enjoy wide-ranging views of the Wakatipu Basin. From here you can see the rugged **Remarkables**, a jagged mountain range that drops dramatically down to Lake Wakatipu.

ARROWTOWN

Back at the bottom of the mountain, turn left on to Malaghans Road and resume your journey to **Arrowtown** ❷. Make a stop along Dalefield Road about 1km (²/₃ mile) past the Coronet Peak turn-off to visit the cluster of art galleries situated here.

Continuing on, watch out for **Millbrook Resort** (Malaghans Road, Arrowtown; tel: 03 441 7000; www.millbrook.co.nz; *see p.118*), a stylish hotel

complex with an 18-hole golf course designed by one of New Zealand's top golfers, left-hander Bob Charles. It's also your cue to take the next left on to Berkshire Street, which leads into Arrowtown via its leafy main street.

Buckingham Street

Leave the car for a while and take a stroll down Buckingham Street, which has the look and feel of a Hollywood movie set and is especially beautiful in autumn. Here you will find artisan stores and souvenir shops, as well as a number of historic landmarks recalling this small town's rich history, among them a monument to the Chinese gold-miners who played an important role in the development of the region.

Those seeking souvenirs of the golden kind should call into **The Gold Shop** (29 Buckingham Street; tel: 03 442 1319; www.thegoldshop.co.nz; daily), which sells jewellery as well as nuggets. Just beyond **The Gold Shop at Athenaeum Hall** (33 Buckingham Street; tel: 03 442 1123) is a map and information board about Arrowtown, with a potted history of the region.

For a more 'hands-on' historical experience, head to the **Lakes District Centennial Museum** (49 Buckingham Street; tel: 03 442 1824; daily 8.30am–5pm; charge). When your history lesson concludes, cross the street to **The Tap**, see ⑪①; a more modern alternative is **Saffron**, see ⑪②.

Further along, located on what is known as the 'Avenue of Trees' (the willow- and sycamore-lined end of Buckingham Street), is Arrowtown's

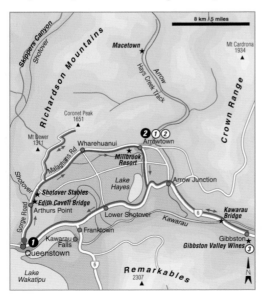

library and beyond that the old schist-built Masonic Lodge and original jail.

Panning for Gold

If you are feeling lucky, a great way to spend half an hour or so is to hire a gold-pan (available from the information centre at 49 Buckingham Street; daily 8.30am–5pm) and try your hand at gold-panning. Just below the village, beyond a long line of car parks, is the Arrow River, where with a bit of time and effort you have a decent chance of garnering a few gold flakes.

Arrowtown Chinese Camp

Another way to gain insight into the hardships of mining a century ago is to walk to the **Arrowtown Chinese Camp** (daily; free), located on the high river bank, near where you entered town. Plum and berry trees surround these hillside huts. Check out Ah-Lums Store at the beginning of the walkway and the humorous Historic Places classification given to an old toilet.

BACK TO QUEENSTOWN

There are several routes out of Arrow-town, but we suggest driving back along Berkshire Street and, instead of turning into Malaghans Road, continue on for a scenic drive past Lake Hayes. At the junction with SH6, turn left and travel for 10km (6 miles), until you reach the Kawarau Bridge, the site of A.J. Hackett's first commercial bungy-jump operation (SH6, Queenstown; www. bungy.co.nz; tel: 03 442 7100; daily summer 9am–5pm, winter 9.30am–

5pm; charge), an option for thrill-seeking visitors.

Gibbston Valley Wines

For a relaxing end to the day head to **Gibbston Valley Wines** (SH6, Queens-town; tel: 03 442 690; www.gvwines. co.nz; charge), see ⑪③, a further 5km (3 miles) along SH6. Tours are held on the hour through the vineyard and winery, finishing with a wine-tasting in the cool of a schist cave.

Although the vineyard's focus is on its internationally recognised pinot noir, other attractions, such as Gibbston Valley Cheesery, where small batches are made with flavours changing subtly with the seasons, are popular. You can sample cheese, then purchase a platter to complement a wine-tasting tray and enjoy it alfresco on tables overlooking the valley, or inside beside a roaring fire.

When you've finished, it's an easy 20-minute drive back to the heart of **Queenstown** via SH6 and SH6A.

Macetown

Upriver from Arrow-town, and reached via either a four-wheel-drive tour with Nomad Safaris (tel: 03 442 6699; www. nomadsafaris.co.nz; daily 8am, 1.30pm) or a hiking track, is Macetown, where hundreds of miners flocked when gold was discovered in the Arrow River in 1862. The town grew rapidly, but the claims were quickly exhausted. Today Macetown is a ghost town with only three of its original buildings still standing.

Food and Drink

① THE TAP
51 Buckingham Street; tel: 03 442 1860; daily noon–late; $$
A good choice for a heart-warming New Zealand country-style lunch in an historic, century-old stone house.

② SAFFRON
Buckingham Street, Arrowtown; tel: 03 442 0131; $$
South Island ingredients are put to good use in Saffron's wide-ranging menu of fusion and world food.

③ GIBBSTON VALLEY WINERY RESTAURANT
SH6, Queenstown; tel: 03 442 6910; $$
Chef Mark Sage focuses on fresh local produce to create a menu that reflects the lifestyle of the region, with dishes such as vine-smoked venison, saddle of rabbit and poached rump of lamb. The ideal complement to the vineyard's wines.

MILFORD SOUND

Last, but certainly not least, this tour takes you to the spectacular Milford Sound, located in Fiordland National Park. Cruise on the fiord and return via the Homer Tunnel and Te Anau to Queenstown.

Maori Masterpiece
Maori legends tell of Tu-te-raki-whanoa, the master carver who crafted the fiords with his adze, beginning in the south and working his way up the coastline to Milford Sound, his *pièce de résistance*.

DISTANCE 598km (371 miles) return
TIME One or two days
START/END Queenstown
POINTS TO NOTE
This trip can be done as a drive or with a tour operator. For car-hire information, *see p.111*. If you are driving yourself, note that it involves an arduous four- to five-hour journey each way. One option is to break this up with an overnight stay in Te Anau *(see p.119)*. It is mandatory for vehicles to carry chains between May and September, and, as there are no other petrol (gas) stations, you will need to fill up your vehicle in Te Anau.

Milford Track
A hearty option is to walk in on the Milford Track, hiking a 54-km (33-mile) route over five days, staying in huts along the way. This trail is so popular that it's fully booked for months in advance, but with some forward planning and a reasonable level of fitness, there is no better way to appreciate fully the Sound.

Milford Sound (a fiord mistakenly thought to be a sound when discovered) is set amid the rainforest of Fiordland National Park. Formed from a sunken glacial valley, it is surrounded by steep bush-clad cliffs that rise to meet the Southern Alps. It is the spectacular final destination of the **Milford Track** *(see left)* but is also accessible by road and can be reached from Queenstown in a long day. A number of tour operators, including **Real Journeys** (tel: 03 249 7416; www.realjourneys.co.nz; charge), offer day trips from **Queenstown ❶**.

TOWARDS THE SOUND

From Queenstown, leave early in the morning and travel south along the edge of **Lake Wakatipu ❷** beneath the rugged **Remarkables** mountain range on **Kingston ❸**, **Athol ❹** and **Mossburn ❺** to **Te Anau** (see ⑪①,② and ③) **❻**, then on up the **Milford Road**, through the plains of Eglinton Valley and into the **Fiordland National Park**.

Waterfalls, forested valleys, granite peaks and spectacular crystal-clear lakes clamour for attention all the way to the 1.2-km long (²⁄₃-mile) **Homer Tunnel**, a remarkable feat of engineering completed over 18 years by a team of just five men using only picks, shovels and wheelbarrows as tools; it descends dramatically to the shores of **Milford Sound ❼**. The iconic Mitre Peak rises in a ceremonial welcome, as you near the end of the 115-km (71-mile) Milford Road.

CRUISING THE SOUND

Organised tours include a cruise on the Sound, but those driving themselves can cruise, too, with **Red Boats** (Milford Wharf, SH94; tel: 03 441 1137; www. redboats.co.nz; daily: summer 9am–3.45pm, winter 9am–1.30pm; charge) or **Real Journeys** (tel: 03 249 7416;

www.realjourneys.co.nz; charge); a less relaxing option is to join a kayak tour.

Highlights

During the cruise, highlights include watching Mitre Peak's three-pointed glaciated slab rise 1,692m (5,551ft) high from the Sound, marvelling at waterfalls such as Lady Bowen Falls, which tumbles 161m (528ft) from a hanging valley, and spotting bottlenose dolphins, fur seals and Fiordland crested penguins near Seal Rock.

If you visit in December, keep an eye open for the beautiful red blossoms of the southern rata, which, like the North Island's pohutukawa, is known as New Zealand's Christmas tree.

Harrison Cove

Depending on time, a recommended inexpensive treat is **Harrison Cove's Underwater Observatory** (tel: 03 441 1137; www.milforddeep.co.nz; daily;

charge), where you can peek below the shallow top layer of tinted fresh water to spy on deepwater species and corals.

Bowen Falls Track

Alternatively, hike the short **Bowen Falls Track**, where you're bound to meet tired but elated Milford Track hikers. For comfort, pack a waterproof jacket, since Fiordland has the highest rainfall levels in the country. Although this seldom dampens the experience, sandflies can, so wear long trousers and cover yourself liberally with insect repellent before leaving your vehicle.

Back to Queenstown

If you are driving yourself, head back the way you came. If you travel to the Sound by organised tour, you will be back in Queenstown by 8–9pm.

Above from far left: the spectacular Milford Sound; photo opportunity near the Sound.

Above: the ideal way to admire the scenery.

Fiord or Sound?
A sound is a slim passage of water connecting either two seas or a sea and a lake. A fiord is a long, narrow inlet of sea tucked between high cliffs.

Food and Drink 🍴

① REDCLIFF CAFÉ
12 Mokonui Street, Te Anau;
tel: 03 249 7431; $$$
In a quaint backstreet cottage, Redcliff does inspired New Zealand dishes.

② LA TOSCANA
108 Milford Road, Te Anau;
tel: 03 249 7756; $$–$$$
A quality pizzeria and spaghetteria:
a taste of Tuscany in Te Anau.

③ CAFÉ LA DOLCE VITA
90 Town Centre, Te Anau; $–$$
tel: 03 249 8895; $–$$
This places serves range of New Zealand dishes plus great coffee.

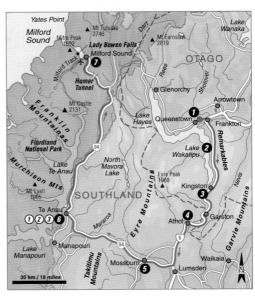

DIRECTORY

A user-friendly alphabetical listing of practical information,
plus hand-picked hotels and restaurants, clearly organised
by area, to suit all budgets and tastes.

A

AGE RESTRICTIONS

The minimum age for driving in New Zealand is 15; however, you must be 21 or over (with a valid driver's licence) to hire a vehicle. The age of consent is 16. You must be 18 years or over to purchase alcohol.

B

BICYCLE HIRE

New Zealand's quiet roads and stunning scenery make it ideal for cycle touring, provided you can cope with numerous hills. The South Island's Canterbury Plains do provide easy flat cycling, as does the city of Christchurch. Here bikes can be hired for NZ$15–35 a day, with some specialist cycle shops arranging more economical rentals from about NZ$200 a month for a standard touring bike in good condition. Ten-speed bikes and tandems can be hired for sightseeing in most cities, while resorts such as Queenstown and Taupo also have mountain bikes for hire. Safety helmets are compulsory, so you might want to bring your own.

Guided cycle tours ranging from six to 18 days are available; on these trips your luggage is transported by van to each lodging along the way. Backpacker transport operators such as Kiwi Experience (tel: 09 366 9830) can arrange bike hire and issue vouchers that allow you to transport your bike on their buses when you're not riding.

BUSINESS HOURS

Business hours are generally Mon–Fri 9am–5pm. Most stores and shops are open Mon–Fri 9am–5.30pm and Sat 10am–1pm. Many also stay open late (until 9pm) one night a week, usually on Thur or Fri; some stores open on Sun. In tourist areas and resorts, shops invariably open on Sun and in the evenings.

Bars, pubs and taverns open Mon–Sat from 11am and close between 11pm and 2am, depending on their licence. Clubs usually open their doors at 7.30–8pm and close around 4am.

C

CRIME AND SAFETY

If you take due care, there is no reason to expect trouble in New Zealand. Take the usual sensible precautions, such as locking your car and never leaving tempting articles visible inside. Make sure camper vans are well secured. Keep valuables in the hotel safe, and don't leave possessions on the beach while you swim. Any theft should be reported immediately to hotel authorities, who will then contact the police.

Drugs offences, particularly if they relate to harder drugs, are treated very seriously. Marijuana is widely available but remains illegal.

While New Zealand is a safe country, it is unwise for a lone woman to walk at night in some big-city areas, such as the 'K' Road nightlife area in Auckland. New Zealand has some

fearsome-looking motorcycle gangs on the roads, but they are unlikely to hassle tourists.

CUSTOMS AND ENTRY REQUIREMENTS

Visas and Passports

All visitors to New Zealand need a passport valid for at least three months beyond the date they intend leaving the country. Citizens of Canada, Ireland, South Africa, the US and several other countries do not require an entry visa if they intend to stay for less than three months. British passport-holders can stay visa-free for six months; Australians can stay indefinitely. To gain entry, visitors must hold fully paid onward or return tickets to a country they have permission to enter and sufficient funds to maintain themselves during their stay in New Zealand (at least NZ$1,000 per person per month).

Everyone arriving in New Zealand must complete an arrival card handed out on the aircraft.

Banned Substances

Animal products, fruit, plant material, or foodstuffs that could contain plant or animal pests and diseases are banned. Heavy fines may be imposed on people caught carrying these. Place anything that fits this description, particularly fruit, in the bins provided on the approach to the immigration area. Drugs, including marijuana and cocaine, are illegal in New Zealand; penalties for possession are heavy and risk affecting your visa status.

Duty on Imported Goods

Goods up to a total combined value of NZ$700 are free of duty and tax, but goods in excess of this may attract both. If you are over 17 you may also take the following into New Zealand free of duty and tax: 200 cigarettes or 250 grams of tobacco or 50 cigars (or a mixture of all three not weighing more than 250 grams); 4.5 litres of wine (equivalent to six standard 750-ml wine bottles) or 4.5 litres of beer and three 1,125-ml bottles of spirits or liqueur. There is no restriction on the import or export of foreign or local currency.

Visitors to New Zealand may purchase duty-free goods, which are not subject to local taxes, from airport duty-free shops upon arrival and departure. Duty-free stores in central Auckland, Wellington and Christchurch deliver purchases to aircraft departure lounges.

ELECTRICITY

230V/50Hz AC is standard. Most hotels have sockets for 110V AC electric razors. The country uses Australasian/Pacific-model plugs with three flat pins.

EMBASSIES AND CONSULATES

The following is a list of the main consular offices in New Zealand:

Australia: 72–6 Hobson Street, Thorndon, Wellington; tel: 04 473 6411; www.australia.org.nz.

Canada: 61 Molesworth Street (PO Box 12049), Wellington; tel: 04 473 9577; www.wellington.gc.ca.

Ireland: Level 7, Citigroup Building, 23 Customs Street East, Auckland; tel: 09 977 2252; www.ireland.co.nz.

UK: 44 Hill Street, Thorndon (PO Box 1812), Wellington; tel: 04 924 2888; www.britain.org.nz.

US: 29 Fitzherbert Terrace, Thorndon (PO Box 1190), Wellington; tel: 04 462 6000; newzealand.usembassy.gov.

EMERGENCIES

Dial 111 for emergency calls to police, fire or ambulance services. Emergency numbers for doctors, dentists, hospitals and local authorities are given in the front of local telephone directories and posted in telephone boxes. Police control call-outs for search-and-rescue services in the bush.

Fire Hazards

Fire poses a constant threat to New Zealand's natural beauty. In summer, scrub and grass are tinder-dry, and the slightest spark can start a blaze. Do not throw matches or cigarettes from car windows, and don't light fires in restricted areas. Beach barbecues are tolerated as long as you remain a safe distance from trees, but be sure to shelter the fire well from sea breezes – a chance cinder can set a whole bush-bound coast alight. Always extinguish a fire carefully by dousing it with water or covering it with earth. Glass can concentrate the sun's rays and start fires; store empty bottles in the shade and take them with you when you leave.

G

GAY AND LESBIAN TRAVELLERS

New Zealand is not generally a homophobic country, although prejudice may persist in smaller towns. The country has a history of enlightened laws relating to human rights. Homosexuality ceased to be categorised as a criminal offence in 1986, and the age of consent was set at 16 (the same as for heterosexuals).

There are lots of facilities and activities in New Zealand catering for gay, lesbian and bisexual travellers, including Gay Ski Week in Queenstown and the Great Party weekend in Wellington. For further information, contact Gay Tourism New Zealand (tel: 04 917 9176; email: info@gay tourismnewzealand.com) or check out the Gay Travel New Zealand website www.gaytravel.co.nz.

GUIDES AND TOURS

A wide choice of escorted package tours are available. These include fly/drive arrangements (with or without accommodation), camper or motorhome hire, fully escorted coach holidays (North Island, South Island, or both), escorted budget coach holidays, farm holidays, trekking holidays and ski packages.

'Flightseeing' in a light aircraft is one of the pleasures of a New Zealand

holiday. It is especially recommended for the outstanding scenic areas of Rotorua, Mount Cook, the Fox and Franz Josef glaciers, Queenstown and Milford Sound. Alpine flights use special planes with retractable skis for landing on snow and ice.

H

HEALTH CARE

Both public and private health services are of a high standard in New Zealand. Hotels and motels usually have a doctor on call, and doctors are listed separately at the front of telephone directories. Medical services are not free, except as a result of an accident, so you are strongly advised to arrange health insurance in advance. In the case of an accident, all visitors are entitled to compensation, covering expenses such as doctor's fees and hospitalisation. New Zealand has reciprocal health agreements with Australia and the UK, but not with any other countries.

Insects and Poisonous Creatures

You don't have to worry about venomous creepy-crawlies in New Zealand. The only poisonous spider, the katipo, is rare and retiring, and there are no snakes. But there is a flying pest that delivers a painful, itchy bite: the gnat-sized sandfly. It is prevalent on the West Coast of the South Island. Keep sandflies at bay with insect repellent. The European wasp, with its yellow-and-black-striped abdomen, has colonised New Zealand

and become a problem in some bush areas. Hikers should carry anti-histamine medication as a precaution.

Sunburn

Guard against sunburn: use a sunscreen lotion of at least factor 15, if you're out of doors for any length of time in the summer, or in alpine areas at any time of year.

Pharmacies

Chemists (pharmacies) usually open 9am–5.30pm Mon–Thur, until 9pm on Fri, and also on Sat morning. The addresses and phone numbers of emergency chemists (for after-hours service) are posted on the doors of all pharmacies.

Drinking Water

New Zealand has an excellent public water supply. Tap water is safe to drink.

HOLIDAYS

The major public holidays are:
1 and 2 Jan: New Year
6 Feb: Waitangi Day
Mar/Apr: Good Friday, Easter Monday
25 Apr: Anzac Day
June: Queen's Birthday (first Mon)
Oct: Labour Day (fourth Mon)
25/26 Dec: Christmas, Boxing Day

L

LAUNDRY/DRY CLEANING

The majority of motels and some hotels have self-service laundry facili-

Extra Holidays
When Christmas, Boxing Day or New Year's Day falls on a Saturday or Sunday, the public holiday is observed on the following Monday. Also, each province holds a holiday on its own anniversary. These range through the year and can vary, so it's worth checking with an authority such as Tourism New Zealand (www.new zealand.com) before you depart.

ties. Large hotels provide laundry and dry-cleaning services. At local laundries and dry cleaners your clothing will usually be returned to you in 48 hours, although you can generally pay more for a speedier service.

M

MAPS

Tourist offices and car-hire companies distribute free maps. The New Zealand Automobile Association also produces regional maps and excellent district maps; a nominal sum is charged for North and South Island maps. Hema Maps, Wises Maps and the Shell Road Atlas are also well produced and widely available.

MEDIA

Newspapers and Magazines

Mass-circulation daily newspapers are produced in New Zealand's main centres. *The Herald* in Auckland is the North Island's largest circulation paper, while *The Press* in Christchurch is the South Island's largest. There are also local daily papers published in provincial centres and larger towns. International papers and magazines can be found in large bookstores in the main cities.

The Listener, a weekly news magazine, publishes a television and radio guide as well as articles on the arts and social issues. *Metro* and *North and South*, both published in Auckland, provide lively, informative and topical

features. International publications are widely available.

Television

The better-standard hotels may feature CNN on Sky television; otherwise, television consists of five free commercial channels, none of which is very exciting. Commercials proliferate, along with many overseas-made repeats and some local content.

Radio

National Radio is the best station for news, current events and quality programming; numerous other stations cater to all tastes. The BBC World Service is easy to pick up throughout the country, and presents news and current events to a high standard, albeit from a distant part of the planet.

MONEY

Currency

New Zealand operates a decimal currency system, with one dollar made up of 100 cents. Coins come in denominations of 10¢, 20¢, 50¢, NZ$1 and NZ$2. Notes come in NZ$5, NZ$10, NZ$20, NZ$50 and NZ$100 denominations.

Banking Hours

These are usually 9.30am–4.30pm Mon–Fri. Some branches open on Sat until 12.30pm.

Credit Cards

Internationally recognised credit cards are widely accepted, and major curren-

Goods and Service Tax
A 12.5 percent Goods and Service Tax (GST), generally included in the quoted price (except with trade goods), is slapped onto virtually everything.

cies such as US dollars, UK pounds and Australian dollars can be readily changed at banks.

International credit cards encoded with a PIN number may be used to withdraw cash from automatic teller machines (ATMs), which are widely available in main shopping centres and suburban malls. Check with your bank before departure to ensure this facility is available to you.

NB: Note that 'Smart Cards', which often have no magnetic strip, are not universally accepted in New Zealand, so contact you card provider for further information prior to your trip.

Traveller's Cheques
Traveller's cheques can also be cashed at banks, bigger hotels and tourist-orientated shops.

P

POLICE

New Zealand police generally do not carry weapons, and you'll find them approachable and helpful.
See also Emergencies, p.104.

POST OFFICES

Main post offices (or post shops, as they are known) sell stationery as well as offering postal and, in many cases, banking services. In rural areas the general store doubles as the post office. It costs NZ\$1.50 to send postcards or aerograms to anywhere in the world. International airmail envelopes cost

NZ\$1.50 to Australia and NZ\$2 to the rest of the world. Domestic mail is divided into first- (FastPost) and second-class (Standar) levels.

R

RELIGION

New Zealand has no state Church, but Christianity is the dominant religion. Protestants outnumber Catholics. The daily papers give details of addresses and times of services.

S

SMOKING

Smoking is not permitted in any restaurants, bars or public buildings in New Zealand.

T

TELEPHONES

Landlines and Public (Pay) Phones
Calls made on private phones are vastly cheaper than those made on public (pay) phones. Local calls from private phones are free to other landlines.

Coin-operated phones are rare in New Zealand, although a few remain at airports and railway stations. Card-operated public phones with trunk (toll) and international direct dialling (IDD) are located throughout the country.

Phone cards are readily available from post offices, supermarkets and

Population
New Zealand has 4 million people, mostly of British descent, with the largest minority (about 12 percent) being Maori of Polynesian origin. New Zealanders are sometimes called 'Kiwis' after the flightless bird that is the country's unofficial national symbol (not after the small furry fruit that also shares the Kiwi name!) You may also hear the term *Pakeha*, which is Maori term for Europeans.

petrol stations in denominations of NZ$5, NZ$10, NZ$20 and NZ$50.

Dialling Codes

The country code for New Zealand is 64. To call abroad, first dial the international access code, 00, then the country code.

Mobile (Cell) Phones

Cell phones operate on GSM and 3G networks, provided by Vodafone (www.vodafone.com) and Telecom (www.telecom.co.nz). You might consider hiring a mobile phone on arrival in New Zealand, or buying prepaid phone cards, available in Vodafone and Telecom shops.

TIME

New Zealand is one of the first places in the world to see the new day, 12 hours ahead of GMT (Greenwich Mean Time). In summer New Zealand uses 'daylight saving', with clocks put forward one hour to GMT+13. Daylight saving begins on the last Sunday in September and ends on the first Sunday of the following April, when clocks are put back to GMT+12.

TIPPING

Tipping is a novelty in New Zealand. Taxi drivers do not expect tips, and service charges are not added to hotel or restaurant bills. Leaving a few dollars after a meal in a reasonable-quality city restaurant will be appreciated, if the service has been good.

TOILETS

Toilets for public use are found in hotel lobbies, shopping centres, large stores, restaurants, museums, cinemas and pubs. Built-up areas have clearly marked public 'rest rooms'; they are also located in most picnic spots along main roads and at the most popular beaches.

TOURIST INFORMATION

Within New Zealand

New Zealand has an established network of visitor information centres known as i-SITES.

Outside New Zealand

Tourism New Zealand maintains marketing and information offices in the following countries:

Australia: Level 8, 35 Pitt Street, Sydney, NSW 2000; tel: 02 9247 5222.
UK: New Zealand House, 80 Haymarket, London SW1Y 4TQ; tel: 020 7930 1662.
US: Suite 300, 501 Santa Monica Boulevard, Santa Monica, CA 90401; tel: 866 639 9325.

TRANSPORT

Getting to New Zealand

From Australia: Frequent direct flights operated by Air New Zealand and Qantas link Sydney and Auckland each day. Recent developments have seen flight frequency increase, with more services flown by B737 aircraft. These days, Australian airlines view New Zealand as virtually a domestic destin-

ation. The same view applies vice versa – though obviously you need appropriate documents to travel between the two countries. Qantas and Air New Zealand offer direct flights to Auckland from major Australian cities, as well as direct flights to Christchurch and Wellington from Brisbane, Melbourne and Sydney. Freedom Air, an Air New Zealand subsidiary, also links centres on each side of the Tasman Sea.

From North America: Auckland is linked with Los Angeles by direct flights, taking slightly less than 16 hours, on average. Several connections a day run from Auckland to Wellington or Christchurch. New Zealand can also be reached with an additional one or two stops in the Pacific. It can be reached from New York City in just two stops and from San Francisco in one stop.

From the UK: Regular weekly flights operate by airlines including Air New Zealand, Qantas and various Asian carriers from London to New Zealand with one, two or three stops en route. Since the flight lasts at least 24 hours, the cheapest ticket may not be the best deal – it may involve more than one airline and two or more stops, typically requiring you to change aircraft (and possibly airlines) in Singapore, Hong Kong, Sydney or Los Angeles.

Airports

Auckland (AKL) International is 22km (13½ miles) south of the city centre. Transport to city by taxi or bus (45 mins).
Christchurch (CHC) International

is 10km (6 miles) northwest of the city centre. Transport to city by taxi or bus (25 mins).
Wellington (WLG) International is 8km (5 miles) southeast of the city centre. Transport to city by taxi or bus (15 mins).

Long-haul international flights generally land in Auckland. Trans-Tasman flights from Australia also serve Wellington, Auckland and Christchurch, with additional direct air links between Australia and smaller centres such as Queenstown, Hamilton, Dunedin and Palmerston North. A departure tax of NZ$25 applies to everyone over the age of 12 leaving the country and can be paid in cash or by credit card.

Domestic Flights

Air New Zealand is the primary domestic carrier, with Qantas and Pacific Blue competing on main trunk routes. A number of smaller companies serve provincial towns. There are frequent flights from main centres, provincial towns and resort areas.

Before departure, overseas tourists can buy an Air New Zealand Airpass, valid for multiple flights within specific periods of time. This lets travellers fly with the more generous international baggage allowance than normal.

Buses

Local **buses** run according to a published timetable. Fares are calculated according to the number of 'sections' travelled. Some city shuttle buses have 'honesty boxes', into which you drop the required amount. (Wellington has

electric trains – called 'units' – that travel to the northern suburbs.)

Coaches provide countryside service. They are not normally air-conditioned but are heated in winter. The main national coach providers are InterCity (www.intercity.co.nz) and Newmans (www.newmanscoach.co.nz). Budget-priced backpacker coaches such as Kiwi Experience (www.kiwiexperience.com) and Magic Bus (www.magicbus.co.nz) also cover major routes.

A number of coach companies offer **passes** along the routes they operate, either with unlimited stops along a fixed line or a certain number of travel days within a set time-frame. The Travelpass (www.travelpass.co.nz) allows unlimited coach travel as well as one ferry and one train journey. Members of the Youth Hostels Association are eligible for 15 percent discounts on coaches.

Trains

New Zealand offers three scenic long-distance rail services. For full information, contact Tranz Scenic, tel: 04 495 0775; www.tranzscenic.co.nz. Here is a rundown of standard one-way adult fares:

Overlander (Auckland–Wellington), NZ$109.

TranzCoastal (Christchurch–Picton), around NZ$93.

TranzAlpine (Christchurch–Greymouth), NZ$139.

If you are a member of the Youth Hostels Association, ask the Association for information about special rail discounts that may be available.

Ferries

The North and South Islands are linked by both passenger and vehicular ferries, which depart frequently. Stewart Island and Great Barrier Island are also connected by ferry, with less frequent daily departures.

Driving

Road Conditions: roads are generally good, and light traffic in remoter parts of the country makes driving a pleasure, although roads can be torturously windy. Auckland often has traffic jams outside of peak hours due to the ongoing and extensive upgrading of its road infrastructure.

Rules and Regulations: provided you hold a valid overseas driver's licence or an international driving permit, you can drive in New Zealand for up to one year before you are required to apply for a New Zealand licence. You must be able to prove you hold a valid overseas licence and drive only those types of vehicles for which you were licensed in your country of origin. Carry your licence or permit with you whenever you are driving.

Traffic keeps to the left. Seat belts are compulsory for all passengers. Helmets are compulsory for motorcyclists and sidecar passengers. Maximum speed limits are 50km/h (30mph) in built-up areas unless otherwise indicated, 100km/h (60mph) on open roads. Road hazards include slips, rock falls, possums, quail, flocks of sheep and herds of cows, so go carefully. If you encounter animals, take your time and edge

through them, or get someone to walk ahead to clear a path for the vehicle.

Note that New Zealand has a bizarre and unique road rule that bewilders the uninitiated and has caused more than one visitor to have an accident: you must yield to every vehicle approaching or crossing from your right. This means that even when you are making a simple left-hand turn, a car facing you coming from the opposite direction has the right of way. If you are hiring a car, ask the hire company to explain this peculiar rule fully before you start out – knowledge of it may help save your vehicle or even your life.

Fuel Costs: fuel is generally cheaper in cities than it is in country areas.

Roadside Assistance: the New Zealand Automobile Association offers free services and privileges to members of accredited overseas motoring organisations. It also handles vehicle insurance. Through the Association you can make reservations for accommodation and the inter-island ferry. See its website, www.nzaa.co.nz, or contact one of the following offices: Auckland: 99 Albert Street, tel: 09 377 4660; Wellington: 342–52 Lambton Quay, tel: 04 931 9999; Christchurch: 210 Hereford Street, tel: 03 964 3650.

Car Hire: to rent a car you will need an approved national or international driving licence. The minimum age is 21, and drivers under 25 sometimes have to pay more for insurance. Major international firms such as Avis, Hertz and Budget have offices in New Zealand, but local firms can often offer cheaper deals. Hire cars range from NZ$40–120 per day, with rates fluctuating seasonally and varying according to the length of rental. Camper vans cost from NZ$90 or less in low season to NZ$225 for a six-berth in high season.

Note, however, that even if you take out a collision-damage waiver, you can still end up paying for the first NZ$500 or NZ$1,000 of any damage to your hire vehicle – whether you are responsible for the accident or not. Some firms let you take out extra insurance to reduce your exposure to this insidious charge.

Chauffeur-driven vehicles are available for short or long trips. Taxi companies also provide the services of experienced driver-guides. Rates usually include basic mileage plus the driver's living expenses and vary according to the number of passengers.

VACCINATIONS

No vaccination certificates are needed for entry into New Zealand. However, if within three weeks of your arrival you develop any sickness such as a skin rash, fever and chills, diarrhoea or vomiting, you should consult a doctor *(see Health Care, p.105)*.

VISAS AND PASSPORTS

See Customs and Entry Requirements, p.103.

Accommodation in New Zealand ranges from five-star city hotels and luxury country lodges to low-cost backpacker hostels. The country's top hotels – all the well-known chains are represented – are comparable to those anywhere in the world. Serviced apartments and all-suite hotels start from about NZ$700 a week. Luxury lodges, usually compact and distinctive mansions or custom-designed villas of exceptional quality, offer world-class service and sublime surroundings at NZ$400–1,000 a night. Backpackers are served by more than 250 hostels, some in settings that are just as splendid as those enjoyed by more expensive establishments; rates start at NZ$15 per person for a shared room.

Auckland

Ascott Metropolis

1 Courthouse Lane; tel: 09 300 8800; www.the-ascott.com; $$$–$$$$$

Housed within a Manhattan-style skyscraper, the Ascott Metropolis offers apartment-style suites, with stylish muted contemporary decor and breathtaking harbour views. Facilities include an indoor pool and fitness suite.

Heritage Auckland

35 Hobson Street; tel: 09 379 8553; www.heritagehotels.co.nz; $$$–$$$$

A top-class hotel in a mid-city Auckland location near the Sky City casino and within walking distance of Viaduct Harbour and the Aotea Centre. The building was once an old department store, and its glory days are back. Health club and fine restaurant.

Parnell Village Motor Lodge

2 St Stephens Avenue, Parnell; tel: 09 377 1463; www.parnell motorlodge.co.nz; $$

Choose between elegant Victorian rooms and modern apartments near the shops in Parnell, five minutes from downtown Auckland.

Skycity Hotel and Skycity Grand Hotel

Corner of Victoria and Federal streets; tel: 09 363 6000; www.skycity.co.nz; $$$–$$$$

The Skycity Hotel is located within the Skycity casino and theatre complex, with its 18 bars, cafés and restaurants and the Sky Tower. The Grand is a more upmarket, luxurious oasis that includes the fine Dine by Peter Gordon restaurant (see p.120), plus gym, pool and spa. The buildings face each other in the heart of downtown Auckland.

Around Auckland

Gulf Harbour Lodge

164 Harbour Village Drive, Whangaparaoa Peninsula; tel: 09 428 1118; www.gulfharbourlodge.com; $$$

On Hauraki Gulf, one hour's drive north of the city, this canal-side lodge has a distinctly Mediterranean feel.

Price guide for a double room with bathroom for one night:	
$$$$$	over NZ$350
$$$$	NZ$250–350
$$$	NZ$150–250
$$	NZ$100–150
$	below NZ$100

Country Club facilities include golf course, tennis and squash courts, heated pool and gymnasium. Daily ferry to Auckland's city centre.

Peace and Plenty Inn

6 Flagstaff Terrace, Devonport; tel: 09 445 2925; www.peace andplenty.co.nz; $$$–$$$$

Set in the lovely, historic harbourside village of Devonport, Peace and Plenty, only a 10-minute ferry ride to Auckland's city centre. Five spacious guest suites, each providing king-and queen-sized beds and high-quality bed linens, and delights from the colonial era including deep claw-foot baths, cast-iron fireplaces and polished kauri floors. Gourmet breakfast is served in sunny breakfast room or alfresco overlooking tropical garden of palms, frangipani and hibiscus blooms.

Waitakere Estate

573 Scenic Drive, Waiatakere Ranges; tel: 09 814 9622; www.waitakere estate.co.nz; $$$–$$$$

A private paradise surrounded by rainforest, perched 240m (800ft) above sea level. The original builder of the hotel, which started life as a family home, had to cut his way through bush to reach the spot where it now stands. The 17 suites have modern facilities, a library and kauri lounge. Gorgeous views over Auckland and the Hauraki Gulf.

Northland

Aloha Seaview Resort Motel

32–6 Seaview Road, Paihia; tel: 09 402 7540; www.aloha.co.nz; $–$$$

Self-contained one- and two-bedroom apartments in 2ha (5 acres) of native bush and subtropical garden. There is a peaceful atmosphere and breathtaking sea views, despite the complex being just a short walk to the shops and waterfront of Paihia.

Edgewater Palms Apartments

8–10 Marsden Road, Paihia; tel 09 402 0090; www.edgewater apartments.co.nz; $$$$–$$$$$

Upmarket self-contained apartments with saltwater pool and spa in an attractive waterfront location close to the vibrant wharf.

Kingfish Lodge Resort

Whangaroa Harbour; tel: 09 405 0164; www.kingfishlodge.co.nz; $$$$$

Situated around 30 minutes from Kerikeri, this secluded lodge with 12 rooms is accessible only by sea or air. All rooms are near the water's edge, with spectacular views from private balconies. Activities include diving, canoeing, fishing and winery cruises. Bar and restaurant.

Orongo Bay Homestead

45 Aucks Road, RD 1, Russell; tel: 09 403 7527; www.the homestead.co.nz; $$$$$

Erected c.1860, this building (in 7 ha/ 17 acres) of lawns with views to the Bay of Islands) once housed New Zealand's first American Consulate. It's now an elite, four-roomed hotel. The restaurant does organic cuisine under an award-winning chef. Wheelchair access.

Coromandel Peninsula

Brian Boru Hotel
Corner of Richmond and Pollen streets, Thames; tel: 07 868 6523; $–$$

A central, convenient place to stay in Thames, this hotel has standard rooms and motel-style units.

Rotorua

Millennium Rotorua
Corner of Eruera and Hinemaru streets; tel: 07 347 1234; www. millenniumrotorua.co.nz; $$$

Deluxe hotel in the middle of town. Ask for a room overlooking the Polynesian Pools and Lake Rotorua, as there are great views from the balcony. Facilities include a gym and pool.

Princes Gate Hotel
1057 Arawa Street; tel: 07 348 1179; www.princesgate.co.nz; $$–$$$

Attractive old colonial-style hotel, built at the end of the 19th century, close to the Polynesian Pools. An elegant retreat.

Rydges Rotorua
272 Fenton Street; tel: 07 349 0099; www.rydges.com/rotorua; $$$

The large, traditionally styled Rydges has panoramic views of Lake Rotorua and is within walking distance of the main shopping area. Restaurants, bar and heated rooftop pool.

Solitaire Lodge
Ronald Road, Lake Tarawera; tel: 07 362 8208; www.solitairelodge.co.nz; $$$$$

Nestled in bushland on a private peninsula 25 minutes from Rotorua, this de-luxe lodge with ten suites has great views of the lake and Mount Tarawera.

Sudima Hotel
1000 Eureka Street; tel: 07 348 1174; www.sudimahotels.com; $$–$$$

Strategically placed opposite the Polynesian Spa, this hotel has superb views of the lake and thermal areas. Within walking distance of Rotorua centre.

Wylie Court Motor Lodge
345 Fenton Street; tel: 07 347 7879; www.wyliecourt.co.nz; $$–$$$

Standard and executive suites, plus outdoor heated swimming pools set in 1ha (2 acres) of gardens. Restaurant open daily. Wheelchair access. 36 units.

Taupo

Huka Lodge
271 Huka Falls Road; tel: 07 378 5791; www.hukalodge.co.nz; $$$$$

Regularly rated as one of the best hotels in the world, the 1920s Huka Lodge is the height of understated luxury, around an hour's drive from Rotorua. It is set within extensive grounds above the Huka Falls, with 20 individual suites dotted among trees by the Waikato River. Fine restaurant. Wheelchair access.

Suncourt Hotel
14 Northcroft Street; tel: 07 378 8265; www.suncourt.co.nz; $$$

This 52-room complex offers a range of accommodation from studio units to two-bedroom units, 40 of which

provide uninterrupted views of Lake Taupo and the mountains of Tongariro National Park.

Terraces Hotel
80–100 SH5, Napier-Taupo Highway; 07 378 7080; www.terraceshotel. co.nz; $$$–$$$$$

This historic Taupo landmark first opened its doors to visitors in 1889 and has been renovated to offer contemporary style and comfort. All rooms have en-suite bathrooms, flat-screen Sky television and internet access plus views of the thermal valley or Lake Taupo.

Wellington

James Cook Hotel Grand Chancellor
147 The Terrace; tel: 04 499 9500; www.ghihotels.com; $$$–$$$$

With entrances on both the Terrace and Lambton Quay, this large, luxurious hotel straddles the premier shopping precinct and the principal commercial districts. Wheelchair access.

Stillwater Lodge
24 Mana Esplanade, Paremata; tel: 04 233 6628; www.stillwater lodge.co.nz; $

Bargain basement backpackers' beach paradise, around 20 minutes north of Wellington on the beachfront.

Tinakori Lodge Bed and Breakfast
182 Tinakori Road; tel: 04 939 3478; www.tinakori lodge.co.nz; $$

This appealing bed-and-breakfast place is handy for rail links, the Botanic Garden and restaurants in the historic Thorndon area. Serves a scrumptious breakfast buffet, too.

The Wellesley
218 Maginnity Street; tel: 04 474 1308; www.thewellesley.co.nz; $$$$

Situated near Parliament and some of Wellington's best shopping streets, the Wellesley boutique hotel accommodates guests in a magnificently restored heritage building.

Wharekauhau Country Estate
Western Lake Road, RD 3, Featherston, Pirinoa; tel: 06 307 7581; www.wharekauhau.co.nz; $$$$$

Pronounced 'Forry-ko-ho', this award-winning lodge sits on a sweeping expanse of ruggedly beautiful land along Palliser Bay, a 90-minute drive east of Wellington. Modelled on an Edwardian country mansion, the main house has a grand hall, massive fireplaces and sumptuous furnishings. Wheelchair access.

Martinborough

Peppers Hotel Martinborough
The Square; tel: 02 8062 5000; www. peppers.co.nz/Martinborough; $$$$$

Around 75 minutes drive east of Wellington, this elegant colonial hotel was established in 1882, as a stopping point for prosperous travellers between the area's isolated sheep stations. It's now a gorgeous retreat – beautifully styled and elegant – with a good restaurant that serves European cuisine. Also wireless internet access and all mod cons.

Above from far left: guest room at Auckland's Ascott Metropolis (see p.112); drinks at the bar at the Sudima Hotel in Rotorua.

Camping
Since much of New Zealand's appeal lies out of doors, camping is a great way to see the country. Many people rent a caravan (trailer) or motor home (camper van). Luxury vehicles come with heating, toilets, fridges, cookers and kitchen utensils. Holiday Parks (motor camps) near main resorts are well maintained and come with electricity and toilet, kitchen and laundry facilities. Some offer cabins; for these you provide your own blankets, linen and cutlery. Prices vary according to standards and season. Advance reservations are necessary during the peak season (Dec–Apr), and it's a good idea to book as far in advance as possible.

Picton and Blenheim

Harbour View Motel

30 Waikawa Road, Picton; tel: 03
573 6259; www.harbourviewpicton.
co.nz; $$

As the name suggests, every room has
a full lookout on to the waterfront, plus
a private balcony and fully equipped
kitchen. A short stroll leads to the
water's edge and the heart of Picton.

Hotel d'Urville

52 Queen Street, Blenheim; tel: 03
577 9945; www.durville.com; $$$$

Situated within an historic building in
the town centre, this boutique hotel with
luxurious, individually themed rooms
has a reputation for unstuffy elegance.
Signature restaurant d'Urville's is open
for breakfast, lunch and dinner. Wheel-
chair access. 10 rooms.

Sennen House

9 Oxford Street, Picton; tel: 03 573
5216; www.sennenhouse.co.nz;
$$$–$$$$

This bed-and-breakfast and self-
catering apartment accommodation is
set inside an historic Picton manor that
has been sympathetically restored. Each
apartment or suite has its own entrance,
en-suite bathroom, satellite television
and comfortable beds with pure cotton
percale linen. A generous daily breakfast
hamper is included in the tariff.

Kaikoura

Blue Seas Motel

222 The Esplanade; tel: 03 319 5441;
www.blueseasmotel.co.nz; $$–$$$

Right on the seafront, this motel offers
a choice of 13 self-contained units
with sea and/or mountain views. All
come with fully equipped kitchens.

Dylans Country Cottages

268 Postmans Road; tel: 03 319
5473; www.lavenderfarm.co.nz; $$

Peaceful, private self-contained country
cottages nestled on a fragrant lavender
farm at the foot of Mount Fyffe. Choice
of indoor spa bath or secluded outdoor
courtyard bath – perfect for stargazing.
Breakfast is included in the tariff.

White Morph Motor Inn

92 The Esplanade; tel: 03 319 5014;
www.whitemorph.co.nz; $$–$$$$

Superbly located in a quiet spot on
the waterfront, 20m (66ft) from the
water's edge. The apartments include
luxury hydrotherapy spa studios with
balconies and sea views, garden studios
and spa apartments. Recommended.

Christchurch

Crowne Plaza Christchurch

Corner of Kilmore and Durham
streets; tel: 03 365 7799; www.
crowneplaza.com; $$–$$$$$

This large premier hotel is set by the
Avon River in a strikingly modern
building recognisable by its crenellated
silhouette. Rooms are furnished in the
modern style and many have great views
over the 'Garden City'. Gymnasium and
business centre. Wheelchair access.

The George

50 Park Terrace; tel: 03 379 4560;
www.thegeorge.com; $$$$$

This lovely boutique hotel is situated close to the city centre, with the historic arts centre, museum, casino and theatres within walking distance. Its 53 rooms are decorated in the contemporary style with luxury amenities. Most have park and river views. Excellent restaurant serving Pacific Rim cuisine. Wheelchair access.

Heritage Christchurch
28–30 Cathedral Square; tel: 03 377 9722; www.heritagehotels.co.nz; $$$–$$$$
Guests can choose to stay in the modern Heritage Tower, or in a turn-of-the-century building that has retained its historic charm. Wheelchair access. 176 rooms.

Aoraki/Mount Cook
The Hermitage Hotel
Terrace Road, Aoraki/Mount Cook Village; tel: 03 435 1809; www. hermitage.co.nz; $$$–$$$$$
The Hermitage alpine resort comprises the main Hermitage Hotel, plus the Hermitage Motels and Chalets, offering 214 rooms with views of Aoraki/Mount Cook and the Southern Alps through enormous picture windows. Facilities include a sauna, babysitting service and laundry. The hotel also houses the Panorama restaurant *(see p.85)*, where the chef Franz Blum creates world-class cuisine using local produce.

Arthur's Pass
Bealey Hotel
SH73, Arthur's Pass; tel: 03 318 9277; www.bealeyhotel.co.nz; $$

Located some 12km (8 miles) east of Arthur's Pass, this modern hotel in an historic spot *(see p.87)* offers a small number of motel-style units with basic facilities but spectacular river and mountain views.

Queenstown
Copthorne Lakefront Resort
Corner of Adelaide and Frankton roads; tel: 03 442 8123; www.copthorne lakefront.co.nz; $$$
Four-star accommodation with 241 cosy rooms, many with views of the lake and mountains. Not in the centre of Queenstown but within walking distance of the main shopping area. Shuttle service available.

The Millennium
Corner of Frankton Road and Stanley Street; tel: 03 441 8888; www.millenniumqueenstown.co.nz; $$$–$$$$$
This large centrally located luxury hotel lacks lake views but has excellent facilities, including a gymnasium, sauna and spa. Wheelchair access.

Nugget Point Boutique Hotel
146 Arthur's Point Road; tel: 03 441 0288; www.nuggetpoint.co.nz; $$$$

Price guide for a double room with bathroom for one night:

$$$$$	over NZ$350
$$$$	NZ$250–350
$$$	NZ$150–250
$$	NZ$100–150
$	below NZ$100

Award-winning boutique property just 10 minutes' drive from Queenstown. The suites are impeccably furnished, with the more expensive ones featuring stunning views of the Shotover River and Coronet Peak. Friendly, very competent staff. The Birches restaurant is highly recommended.

Queenstown House

69 Hallenstein Street; tel: 03 442 9043; www.queenstownhouse.co.nz; $$$$–$$$$$

A great little hotel with magnificent lake and mountain views from every room and a hostess who is a local personality. Complimentary New Zealand wines and cheese each evening before dinner. 14 rooms.

Rolleston House YHA Hostel

5 Worcester Boulevard; tel: 03 366 6564; www.yha.co.nz; $

This turn-of-the-20th-century home across from the lovely, historic Arts Centre with its weekend craft markets has been converted into backpacker lodgings. 52 beds.

Rydges Lakeland Resort

38–54 Lake Esplanade, Queenstown; tel: 03 442 7600; www.rydges.com/queenstown; $$$

Queenstown's largest hotel is in an excellent location by the waterfront, a short stroll to Steamer Wharf and into town. There are 255 rooms, most of which have lake or mountain views. Facilities include a spa pool, sauna, heated outdoor pool and several restaurants and bars.

Arrowtown

Arrowfield Apartments

115 Essex Avenue; tel: 03 442 0012; www.arrowfield.co.nz; $$$$$

Arrowfield Apartments offer 22 luxurious one-, two- and three-bedroom apartments with underfloor heating, gas fires and plasma televisions. The apartments also have designer kitchens and bathrooms, garage parking, an indoor heated pool, tennis court and gym.

Millbrook Resort

Malaghans Road; tel: 03 441 7000; www.millbrook.co.nz; $$$$$

Located between Queenstown and Arrowtown, this large, multi-award-winning resort provides luxurious modern accommodation in restored historic buildings. Among the attractions are an 18-hole golf course and alpine views. *See also p.96.*

Hokitika

Beachfront Hotel

111 Revell Street; tel: 03 755 8344; www.beachfronthotel.co.nz; $$–$$$

Located right on the shores of the Tasman Sea in the heart of Hokitika, 30 new, modern de-luxe and executive rooms provide ocean views and are steps from the beach. A further 23 comfortable standard and superior rooms face the main street. On-site restaurant, café and bar.

Country Comfort Shining Star Beachfront Chalets

16 Richards Drive; tel: 03 755 8921; www.shiningstar.co.nz; $–$$

Set among gardens and with an exclusive beach walkway, these chalets are ideal for families and couples wanting space and peaceful surroundings. Full facilities including a sauna, spa pool, BBQ area, children's playground, movie hire and wireless broadband.

Franz Josef Glacier

Glenfern Villas

SH6, Franz Josef Glacier; tel: 03 752 0054; www.glenfern.co.nz; $$$

These luxury self-contained villas are located 3km (2 miles) north of Franz Josef village in a country setting with views of the Southern Alps. There's a choice of either one- or two-bedroom villas; all offer full kitchens, separate bedrooms and generously sized living areas. The two-bedroom villas can sleep up to six people.

Holly Homestead
Bed and Breakfast

SH6, Franz Josef Glacier; tel: 03 752 0299; www.hollyhomestead. co.nz; $$$–$$$$

Set inside a gracious old homestead, this popular bed-and-breakfast place offers comfortable upmarket rooms, a cosy guest lounge and alpine views. The hosts can provide friendly, helpful advice on local activities.

Greymouth

Infinity Eden Lodge

15 Tasman View Road; tel: 03 762 6556; www.infinityedenlodge.co.nz; $$$

Six double guest rooms with en-suite bathrooms and panoramic sea, mountain and bush views. Facilities includ a spa pool, Sky television, internet and a guest-only *table d'hôte* menu.

Fox Glacier

Rainforest Motel

15 Cook Flat Road, Fox Glacier; tel: 03 751 0140; www.rainforest motel.co.nz; $$

Perfect for families, this spacious and clean motel comprises studios and one- and (large) two-bedroom units, all with kitchens, en-suite bathrooms and views of the Southern Alps and local rainforest.

Scenic Circle Glacier
Country Hotel

SH6, Fox Glacier; tel: 03 751 0847; www.scenic-circle.co.nz; $$$

Situated in the heart of Fox Glacier Village, this hotel offers 51 serviced rooms, guest laundry facilities, an internet kiosk, room service, a camera-to-photo kiosk, tourist information and booking service and a restaurant/bar. It's a cosy retreat and very handy for all the outdoor activities Fox Glacier has to offer.

Te Anau

Te Anau Hotel and Villas

64 Lakefront Drive; tel: 03 249 9700; www.teanauhotel.co.nz; $$$–$$$$$

Situated directly on the lakefront, this large hotel has a range of spacious rooms and suites, all furnished in the modern style and many with commanding views of the lake. Facilities include a restaurant/bar, spa pool and sauna. A good stop en route to/from Milford Sound.

Above from far left: country lodge; Edgewater Palms Apartments and pool *(see p.113)*.

You can generally expect a good standard of dining in New Zealand. Chefs have high-quality local ingredients to work with, including fresh fruits and vegetables and an enviable range of freshwater and saltwater fish, game and farmed meat. Servings are often hearty, and in many places a main course may be enough. The list below is not intended to be comprehensive, but instead features our top choices, especially for evening dining, across the country.

Auckland

Antoine's Restaurant

333 Parnell Road, Parnell; tel: 09 379 8756; www.antoinesrestaurant. co.nz; $$$$

Elegant, innovative gourmet restaurant in the heart of Parnell. The menu offers New Zealand cuisine with French undertones. Reserve.

Cibo

91 St Georges Bay Road, Parnell; tel: 09 303 9660; www.cibo.co.nz; $$$

Tucked away in an old chocolate factory, Cibo does Mediterranean plus Asian-influenced cuisine. The well-executed dishes and superb service have kept it at the top for over a decade.

> Price guide for a two-course meal for one with a glass of house wine:
>
> | | |
> |---|---|
> | $$$$ | above NZ$80 |
> | $$$ | NZ60–80 |
> | $$ | NZ$40–60 |
> | $ | below NZ$40 |

Dine by Peter Gordon

Skycity, 90 Federal Street; tel: 09 363 7030; www.skycitygrand.co.nz; $$$

Excellent service and an exciting menu of fusion food served under one of the country's top chefs. Great service too.

Euro

Shed 22, Princes Wharf; tel: 09 309 9866; www.thenourishgroup.co.nz; $$$

Fashionable restaurant that focuses on fresh New Zealand produce. High-quality food and excellent service.

Harbourside Seafood Bar and Grill

1st floor, Ferry Building, 99 Quay Street; tel: 09 307 0556; www. harboursiderestaurant.co.nz; $$$$

Fine dining on the waterfront with wonderful views of the harbour. The seafood is super-fresh and delicious; try the 'Trio', hapuka, kingfish and salmon in one succulent dish.

Observatory Restaurant

Level 52, Sky Tower; tel: 09 363 6000; www.skycityauckland.co.nz; $$$

Venture nearly 200m (660ft) up Auckland's tallest structure to the highest restaurant in the tower for buffet-style New Zealand seafood specialities.

Rice

10–12 Federal Street; tel: 09 359 9113; www.rice.co.nz; $$

This chic, modern restaurant and bar does mouthwatering international cuisine, made from 20 types or derivatives of rice. Try the entrée platter, notably the

barbecue pork and crispy vermicelli endive-like 'witlof' ('white leaf') bites.

SPQR
150 Ponsonby Road, Ponsonby; tel: 09 360 1710; $$$
One of Auckland's best-loved restaurants, SPQR serves New Zealand classics. Recommendations include the lamb and the linguine and clams dish.

Vivace
Level 1, 50 High Street; tel: 09 302 2303; www.vivacerestaurant.co.nz; $$
Italian-inspired food served tapas-style. Good wine list.

Wildfire
Shed 22, Princes Wharf; tel: 09 353 7595; www.wildfirerestaurant.co.nz; $$
Meat and seafood abound in this Mediterranean eatery by the waterfront. Dishes range from tapas to gourmet pizza and wood-fired grills.

Gannets Restaurant
York Street, Russell; tel: 09 403 7990; www.gannets.co.nz; $$$
Popular with the local crowd, Gannets offers a varied menu with lots of seafood and good vegetarian options. Everything is home-made, even the ice cream.

Bistro 1284
1284 Eruera Street; tel: 07 346 1284; www.bistro1284.co.nz; $$$
Attractively set in an historic 1930s building, this restaurant has won numerous awards − including best in the city − for its delicious New Zealand and international cuisine.

Cableway Restaurant
185 Fairy Springs Road; tel: 07 347 0027; www.skyline skyrides.co.nz; $$
Buffets are not normally worth recommending, but the selection here is first-rate, from multitudinous seafood to perfectly roasted meats. A bonus is the ride in the gondola to the hilltop site.

The Bach
2 Pataka Road; tel: 07 378 7856; www.thebach.co.nz; $$$
Superbly fresh New Zealand-inspired cuisine. Favourite dishes include lamp rump and confit of duck. Very popular with the locals.

Boulcott Street Bistro
99 Boulcott Street; tel: 04 499 4199; www.boulcottstreetbistro.co.nz; $$$
This fine restaurant housed in a pretty cottage just off Willis Street has an air of relaxed formality and serves some of New Zealand's finest game and seafood, all stylishly presented.

Citron
270 Willis Street; tel: 04 801 6263; www.citronrestaurant.co.nz; $$$$
Internationally trained Rex Morgan took a gamble on opening a *dégustation* restaurant here, but it's been such a success that nowadays the regulars don't even bother looking at the menu − they know whatever he gives them will be sensational. À la carte also available.

Above from far left: finishing touches; bowl of mussels; vines; delicious New Zealand lamb.

New Zealand Specialities
New Zealand's 'Pacific Rim' cuisine style takes its inspiration from regions and countries such as Europe, Thailand, Malaysia, Indonesia, Polynesia, Japan and Vietnam. For dishes with a distinctly New Zealand style, look out for dishes made with lamb, venison, salmon, crayfish, Bluff oysters, *paua* (abalone), mussels, scallops, kumara, kiwi fruit or tamarillo. Be sure to sample New Zealand's national dessert, pavlova, made from meringue, topped with lashings of fresh whipped cream and seasonal fresh fruit.

Local Wine

New Zealand's long growing season and cool maritime or sub-alpine climate provides ideal conditions for producing wine. New Zealand's major grape growing areas include the sunny eastern regions of Gisborne and Hawke's Bay; Marlborough in the northeast of the South Island; and the sub-alpine valleys of Queens-town and Central Otago. Vineyards are also found in Northland, Auck-land, Martin-borough, Nelson and Canterbury.

Logan Brown Restaurant

192 Cuba Street; tel: 04 801 5114; www.loganbrown.co.nz; $$$$

One of the city's top restaurants, beautifully set in a 1920s bank, this place does contemporary classics using top-quality New Zealand produce. Book in advance to secure a table here. Stylish.

Shed 5 Restaurant & Bar

Shed 5, Queens Wharf; tel: 04 499 9069; www.shed5.co.nz; $$$$

Smart seafood (and meat dishes) by the water in a spacious, well-renovated 1880s wool shed that is now a café, bar and restaurant in one. Popular for relaxed, extended corporate lunches.

The Tasting Room

2 Courtenay Place; tel: 04 384 1159; www.thetastingroom.co.nz; $$–$$$

Located in the heart of the entertainment district, this gastropub specialises in traditional pub fare with a modern twist. The menu is matched with a wide range of good beers.

The Wairarapa

Wendy Campbell's French Bistro

3 Kitchener Street, Martinborough; tel: 06 306 8863; $$$

Owners and hosts Jim and Wendy Campbell fled Wellington to Martinborough in order to establish this small restaurant that specialises in regional produce and serves wonderful local wines. The bistro received some well-deserved publicity, when Oscar-winning actor Adrien Brody dined there and raved about it.

Blenheim

Twelve Trees Restaurant

Allan Scott Wines and Estate, Jacksons Road; tel: 03 572 7123; www.allanscott.com; $$

The menu here showcases Allan Scott's full-bodied wines. Gorgeous indoor/outdoor setting fewer than 10 minutes out of town on the way to the airport.

Christchurch

The Blue Note

20 New Regent Street; tel: 03 379 9674; www.bluenote.co.nz; $$

Great food with a Mediterranean influence, plus live jazz. The ambience is warm; the setting – on the pedestrian-only New Regent Street – is superb.

Indochine

209 Cambridge Terrace; tel: 03 365 7323; www.indochine.co.nz; $$

Some call this the best restaurant in the city. Elaborate, varied pan-Asian menu. Tempting cocktail list, too.

Retour

Corner of Cambridge Terrace and Manchester Street; tel: 03 365 2888; closed Mon; www.retour.co.nz; $$$

Formerly a band rotunda, now a glass-sided restaurant overlooking the Avon River and ideal for a romantic dinner. Premium New Zealand cuisine.

Saggio di' Vino

Corner of Victoria Street and Bealey Avenue; tel: 03 379 4006; $$$

A 'vinothèque', where the food complement the 80+ wines sold by the glass.

Sign of the Takahe

200 Hackthorne Road, Cashmere Hills; tel: 03 332 4052; www.sign ofthetakahe.com; $$$

Silver service and fine dining in a baronial hilltop castle. Serves modern and traditional New Zealand cuisine.

Tiffany's Restaurant

95 Oxford Terrace; tel: 03 379 1350; www.tiffanys.co.nz; $$$

Offering fine wines and the best of regional cuisine, Tiffany's has a picturesque riverside location but is still close to the centre of town. Service is top class. Alfresco lunches here are highly recommended.

Queenstown

The Bathhouse

5 Marine Parade; tel: 03 442 5625; www.bathhouse.co.nz; $$$$

Located in an authentic Victorian bathhouse with scenic views of the waterfront. The romantic old-world ambience belies the innovative fusion cuisine served. Crab cakes with anise plum sauce and the duck poached in five spices are winners.

The Birches

146 Arthur's Point Road; tel: 03 441 0288; www.nuggetpoint.co.nz; $$$$

Located at the luxury Nugget Point Resort, 10 minutes away from downtown Queenstown, the restaurant is well worth the detour. Chef Randall Wadman turns the freshest of New Zealand produce into creative and innovative dishes. The herb-crusted rack of lamb is to die for.

The Bunker

Cow Lane; tel: 03 441 8030; www. thebunker.co.nz; $$$$

This small, stylish restaurant serves simple, fresh, modern cuisine. Reservations are essential.

Lone Star

14 Brecon Street; tel: 03 442 9995; $$

As the name implies, this is a cowboy-themed restaurant, serving North American classics such as burgers, ribs and Dixie chicken. Huge portions.

Minami Jujisei

45 Beach Street; tel: 03 442 9854; $$

Award-winning Japanese restaurant that does traditional dishes with a modern twist.

Roaring Megs Restaurant

53 Shotover Street; tel: 03 442 9676; www.roaringmegs.co.nz; $$-$$$

Renovated goldminer's cottage turned fine restaurant. The house speciality is rack of lamb.

Solera Vino

25 Beach Street; tel: 03 442 6082; $$$

Intimate, romantic restaurant with a Mediterranean ambience and a New Zealand menu. Good wine list.

Tatler Restaurant

5 The Mall; tel: 03 442 8372; www. tatler.co.nz; $$$

Evocatively set in an historic gold-rush-era building. Dishes include Akaroa salmon fillet served with basmati rice.

Above from far left: cake selection at the Sudima Hotel Rotorua *(see p.114)*; haute cuisine at The George *(see p.117)*; fish on the barbie.

Regional Cuisine
Every region of New Zealand has its own gourmet delights. Northland has award-winning cheeses and subtropical fruit. Rotorua is the place for a *hangi* – a traditional Maori feast cooked in an underground oven. Marlborough offers scallops and green lipped mussels; Canterbury the best racks of lamb; and in Bluff, a foodie's world revolves around the biggest, fattest oysters imaginable.

No Smoking
To protect from the adverse health effects of passive smoking, lighting up in bars, cafés and restaurants is prohibited in New Zealand.

CREDITS

Insight Step by Step New Zealand
Written by: Craig Dowling and Donna Blaber
Series Editor: Clare Peel
Cartography Editors: Zoë Goodwin and James Macdonald
Picture Manager: Steven Lawrence
Art Editor: Ian Spick
Production: Kenneth Chan
Photography by: Apa/Andy Belcher 2B, 2M, 2ML, 2MR,2TL, 2TR, 3BL, 3BR, 3ML, 3MR, 4B, 4M, 4T, 5B, 5M, 5T, 6, 9, 11, 12, 16B, 16M, 16MT, 22MM, 24, 24B, 24T, 25B, 25M, 25T, 26, 26B, 27, 28, 30, 31TR, 33, 34, 38TR, 39, 40, 41, 41B, 41M, 42B, 42TL, 44, 44TL, 47, 49, 50, 52, 55, 56B, 57, 58, 58TL, 61, 62–3, 62, 65, 67, 68, 71, 71B, 71M, 75, 76–7, 76T, 78–9, 79, 80, 82, 85, 86, 87, 87B, 87M, 88–9, 88, 88B, 88TL, 89B, 90–1, 90TL, 91, 91B, 91TR, 92, 92TL, 92TR, 93TR, 94TL, 94TR, 95, 96, 98, 98T, 101, 103, 104; Bay of Plenty Tourism 47TR, 102; Donna Blaber 11B, 14TR, 15B, 15TL,18B, 30, 55, 65, 65B, 65M, 66TL, 77T, 78TL, 79TR, 85TL, 79TR, 85TL, 85TR; Canterbury Tourism 8L, 73M, 73TL, 75B, 75TR, 84TR, 106; Destination Rotorua 20b, 49TR, 52–3; Hans Hubler 63TR; Heritage Hotels 61T; iStockPhoto 2BL, 2BR, 4 2nd from top, 8–9, 8BM, 8MR, 10B, 12TL, 14B, 14M, 17B, 18–19, 18M, 18TL, 19TR, 22BL, 22BM, 22ML, 26T, 28B, 28TL, 29TR, 30–1, 31B, 32T, 34-35, 34TL, 42TR, 43TL, 43TR, 44–5, 45TR, 46B, 46TL, 48TL, 53M, 54B, 54T, 58–9, 67TR, 72TL, 73TR, 78B, 81TR, 89TR, 95TL, 100–1; Kelly Tarlton's Antarctic Adventure 33B; Kiwi Encounter 80TL; NZ Tourism 13TR, 36–7, 36B, 36M, 37TR, 38TL, 39TL, 39TR, 40TL, 41TR; NZ Tourism/Adventure Films 6BL, 33B, 109; NZ Tourism/Julian Apse 24T, 28–9; NZ Tourism/Rob Brown 12B; NZ Tourism/ Chris Cameron 25T; NZ Tourism/Ben Crawford 4 3rd from top, 22MR, 46–7, 52TL, 95TR, 97, 100BM, 103, 110; NZ Tourism/Gareth Eyres 35, 40–1, 57T, 86–7, 100MR, 104, 105; NZ Tourism/Arno Gasteiger 59; NZ Tourism/ James Heremaia 8ML, 53b, 82B; NZ Tourism/ Legend Photography 12MT, 50TL; NZ Tourism/Fay Looney 10TL, 83T; NZ Tourism, Chris McLennan 2–3, 6T, 7MR, 12TR, 16–17, 50–1, 51TR, 53TR; NZ Tourism/Hiroshi Nameeda 2BM, 12MB, 22BR, 66B, 70T, 71T, 72TR, 73B, 73MT, 96–7; NZ Tourism/Nick Servian 2M, 33M; NZ Tourism/Gilbert van Reenan 11TL, 11TR; NZ Tourism/Kieran Scott 33T, 36TL, 62M, 64T, 74TL, 75TL, 100MM, 120TR, 121TL, 123; NZ Tourism/Mark Smith; NZ Tourism/Rob Suisted 4 4th from top, 7BR, 7T, 22–3, 27, 56T, 68TL; NZ Tourism/Ian Trafford 4 5th from top, 6BR, 7BL, 10TR, 60T, 69T, 108; NZ Tourism/Scott Venning 30B, 32B, 33MT; NZ Tourism/David Wall 4T, 8M, 44B, 58B; NZ Tourism/Zorb Rotorua 107; Positively Welington 4B, 6MR, 7ML, 61T; Rex Features 82T, 84; Sky Tower 48–9; Southland Tourism 6L, 10M; Te Papa Museum 62TL; Treble Cone Ski 87T; Zorb Rororua 107.

Cover: gettyimages/Pete Turner: main image; Deco/Alamy BL; iStockPhoto BR.
Printed by: Insight Print Services (Pte) Ltd, 38 Joo Koon Road, Singapore 628990

www.insightguides.com

DISTRIBUTION

Worldwide

Apa Publications GmbH & Co. Verlag KG (Singapore branch), 38 Joo Koon Road,
Singapore 628990
Tel: (65) 6865 1600
Fax: (65) 6861 6438

UK and Ireland

GeoCenter International Ltd
Meridian House, Churchill Way West,
Basingstoke, Hampshire, RG21 6YR
Tel: (44) 01256 817 987
Fax: (44) 01256 817 988

United States

Langenscheidt Publishers, Inc.
36–36 33rd Street, 4th Floor,
Long Island City, NY 11106
Tel: (1) 718 784 0055
Fax: (1) 718 784 0640

Australia

Universal Publishers
1 Waterloo Road, Macquarie Park, NSW 2113
Tel: (61) 2 9857 3700
Fax: (61) 2 9888 9074

New Zealand

Hema Maps New Zealand Ltd (HNZ)
Unit D, 24 Ra ORA Drive,
East Tamaki, Auckland
Tel: (64) 9 273 6459
Fax: (64) 9 273 6479

CONTACTING THE EDITORS

We would appreciate it if readers would alert us to errors or outdated information by writing to us at insight@apaguide.co.uk or Apa Publications, PO Box 7910, London SE1 1WE, UK.

INDEX

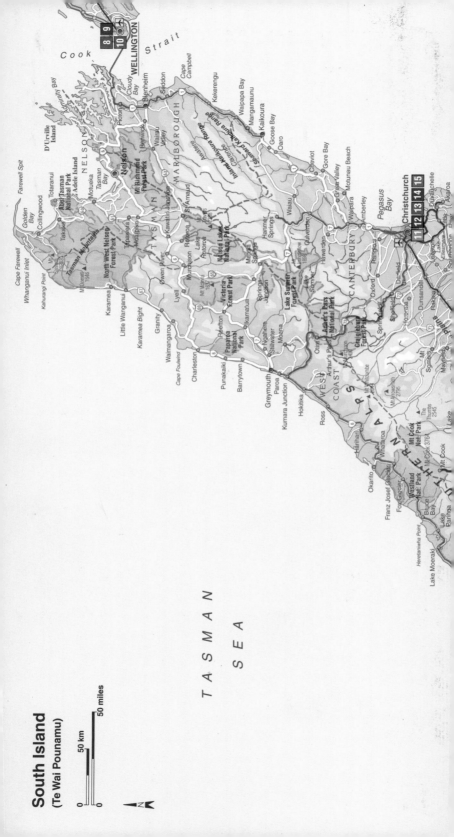